ALL ABOUT

Adam
& Eve

How WE CAME TO BELIEVE
IN GODS, DEMONS, MIRACLES,
& MAGICAL RITES

ROBERT J. GILLOOLY

FOREWORD BY ASHLEY MONTAGU

Prometheus Books
59 John Glenn Drive
Amherst, New York 14228-2197

Cover illustration taken from the *Detroit Free Press*, August 22, 1990.

The publishers have generously given permission to use extended quotations from the following copyrighted works. From *Folklore in the Old Testament*, by Sir James George Frazer. Abridged edition, copyright 1988 by Avenel Books. Published by permission of A. P. Watt Ltd on behalf of Trinity College, Cambridge. From *The Golden Bough: A Study in Magic and Religion*, by Sir James George Frazer. Abridged edition, copyright 1922 by Macmillan Publishing Company, renewed 1950 by Barclays Bank Ltd. Reprinted by permission of the publisher, Simon & Schuster, and by A. P. Watt Ltd. on behalf of Trinity College, Cambridge. From *The Encyclopaedia of Religion and Ethics,* edited by James Hastings. Copyright 1951 by Charles Scribner and Sons. Reprinted by permission of the publisher, T&T Clark Ltd. From "Who Wrote the Bible?" Copyright 1990, December 10, *U.S. News & World Report*. Reprinted by permission of the publisher.

Published 1998 by Prometheus Books

02 01 00 99 98   5 4 3 2 1

Library of Congress Cataloging-in-Publication Data

Gillooly, Robert J.
    All about Adam & Eve : how we came to believe in gods, demons, miracles, & magical rites / Robert J. Gillooly ; foreword by Ashley Montagu.
        p.   cm.
    Includes bibliographical references and index.
    ISBN 1–57392–187–4 (alk. paper)
    1. Religion—Controversial literature. 2. Religions—Controversial literature.
I. Title.
BL2747.G45   1998
200—dc21   97–45193
                                           CIP

Printed in the United States of America on acid-free paper

Contents

List of Illustrations

At Chinchvad, a small town about ten miles from Poona in Western India, there lives a family of whom one in each generation is believed by a large proportion of the Mahrattas to be an incarnation of the elephant-headed god Gunputty. That celebrated deity was first made flesh about the year 1640 in the person of a Brahman of Poona, by name Mooraba Gosseyn, who sought to work out his salvation by abstinence, mortification, and prayer. His piety had its reward. The god himself appeared to him in a vision of the night and promised that a portion of his, that is, of Gunputty's holy spirit should abide with him and with his seed after him even to the seventh generation. The divine promise was fulfilled. Seven successive incarnations, transmitted from father to son, manifested the light of Gunputty to a dark world. The last of the direct line, a heavy looking god with very weak eyes, died in the year 1810. But the cause of truth was too sacred, and the value of the church property too considerable, to allow the Brahmans to contemplate with equanimity the unspeakable loss that would be sustained by a world which knew not Gunputty. Accordingly they sought and found a holy vessel in whom the divine spirit of the master had revealed itself anew, and the revelation has been happily continued in an unbroken succession of vessels from that time to this.

—Sir James G. Frazer, *The Golden Bough*

Foreword

Mr. Gillooly has written a beautiful and important book about that most controversial of issues: religion and God. It is a remarkable achievement, for he has distilled the essence of the conclusions reached by the most distinguished authorities who have spent their lives wrestling with the problem of the origins of the idea of God and religion. The scholars would have been proud of Mr. Gillooly's accomplishment in clarifying so much that they had made available for emendation. The author's coverage of the varieties of religions is both fascinating and enlightening. Indeed, his book provides an education in itself.

The ideas of God and religion are for the most part really inseparable, although in passing it may be of interest to note that there are peoples such as the Australian aborigines, the Bushmen of the Kalahari Desert, the Chinese, Japanese, and others, who have no gods, and some who having had gods, like the Todas of Southern India, have allowed them to degenerate into oblivion.

Religion is a word which most of us, whether we are believers or not, are inclined to think that we fully understand. The truth, however, is that in spite of more than a century-and-a-half of scholarly study of religion, theological, anthropological, archaeological research, and secular inquiry, no one has yet been able to offer a satisfactory definition of this most widely distributed of human institutions. This may be because religion is by far the most complex of institutions. However that may be, what can be said with some degree of confidence is that religion is one of the oldest of humankind's cultural creations. God, by comparison, is a much easier conception to deal with. Here Mr. Gillooly excels in clarifying the origins and nature of this most eventful concept in the history of humankind.

Human beings have been on this earth for at least three million years, and for at least a million and a half years were making stone tools of great ingenuity, a fact which strongly suggests a remarkable ability for problem solving. Since problem solving is of the essence of thinking, it is more than likely that these early ancestors of ours had already been long involved in responding to the feeling that there must be *something* out there which was responsible for *everything*, for what we call "creation." From this it would naturally follow that there must be a creator or creators.

It is interesting that many millennia later this was precisely the argument employed in 1802 by the brilliant English ecclesiastic and theologian William Paley (1743–1805) in his widely read book *Natural Theology; or, Evidences and Attributes of the Deity, Collected from the Appearances of Nature*. If, argued Paley, he had found a watch he would have unhesitatingly known that its intricate mechanism must have been put together by a watchmaker. Clearly, then, the marvelous "Appearances of Nature," must have been assembled by a Supreme Maker, namely God.

To the reader of the first half of the nineteenth century, before Darwin and the advent of modern biology, Paley's view seemed like a compelling argument, as it still does to many in the twentieth century. The only trouble, however, with the watchmaker analogy is that it is unsound. Before Darwin and the theory of evolution it would have been difficult to refute Paley. Indeed it is worth noting here that Darwin, when a student at Cambridge, read Paley's book and was enchanted by it. As he wrote later, in 1859, in the very month in which his own epochal book was published, "I do not think I ever admired a book more than Paley's *Natural Theology*."

It was Darwin, in *The Origin of Species*, who based on his own field work as well as that of others, showed that the true cause of the "Appearances of Nature" was what he termed "natural selection," or to put it briefly, adaptive fitness, namely, the process whereby favorable mutations by increasing the adaptive fitness of the organism enable it to survive and leave a larger progeny than others not so favored. This represents a much more satisfactory explanation of the development of life on this earth than the idea of a creator. Ideas such as Paley's were plausible in their day, but in the light of the laboriously collected facts and experimental evidence accumulated during the last hundred and fifty years, plausibility has been displaced by proof which has made the idea of a creator highly improbable. For the scientist, truth is proof without certainty, for other people, only too often, truth has been certainty without proof.

Among the many excellences of Mr. Gillooly's book is the admirable clarity and balance with which he approaches the examination of some of the oldest and most cherished beliefs of humankind. In the course of his exposition, he pays particular attention to the dominant religion of the Western world, Christianity. In focusing his well-disciplined mind upon what is for many people a controversial subject, the author never for a moment drops his loving care for truth while at the same time maintaining a scrupulous regard for the feelings of the reader who may be challenged by his exposition.

It has been found again and again in the history of human thought that when fundamental religious beliefs have been critically examined, they have been found to be nothing more than myths. History is to a considerable extent the mythology of those who have created it. In short, insofar as verity is concerned, history is not very accommodating. It should always be remembered that mythology is not accountable to reality, that what passes for knowledge is socially constructed, and that the socially constructed myths which have been handed down to us in the form of religion have a spurious validity which is often more compelling than the truth, especially in an environment in which the unreal is often more real than the real. Too often a society's myths constitute the debt it pays for its structural rigidity, the way it pays for the homogeneity of its ideas about itself and the outside world. Under such circumstances it is the course of wisdom neither to believe nor to disbelieve, but to check the facts for oneself. This, again, is where Mr. Gillooly is powerfully helpful.

In all societies myth has played an incomparably powerful role in the lives of its members. No one has put this better than the distinguished anthropologist Bronislaw Malinowski. "Myth" as he put it, "expresses, enhances, and codifies belief; it safeguards and enforces morality; it vouches for the efficiency of ritual and contains practical rules for the guidance of man; myth is thus a vital ingredient of human civilization; it is not an idle tale, but a hard-worked active force; it is not an intellectual explanation or an artistic imagery, but a pragmatic charter of primitive faith and moral wisdom."

And this is what Mr. Gillooly makes so eminently clear. Adam and Eve have come a long way since their misadventure in the Garden of Eden, and in their modern incarnation have, in great numbers, come to know, through works like that of the author, that man was not made in the image of God, but rather that God was made in the image of man.

It is an image which is so confused and destructive that man, almost everywhere on this planet, has become the most self-destructive creature on this earth. That is not what human beings were born to be. It is a very easy "explanation" to blame it all on "Original Sin," or "Innate Depravity," as it was called when I was a boy, and the Sabbath was full of intangible restraints. But that was all part of an orthodoxy that was all mythology, an endemic belief that has done a great deal of harm, affecting most destructively our attitudes toward children. Children in fact are born with all their drives directed toward love and cooperation. If we would understand this, a fact which is fully supported by the findings of the behavioral sciences, we might yet save ourselves from the ominous threat which, like a dark shadow in the sunlight, only too visibly hangs over us all.

It is only through loving that we find identity, and the only true religion is to live as if to live and to love were one. We learn to love by being loved, and such learning should be the way of life in our homes, our schools, and in all our relationships, as well as in our relation to that nature of which we are a part; and above all to learn that while it is good to love thy neighbor as thyself, it is not enough: we must love others *more* than we love ourselves, and finally, that a good deed is the best prayer, a loving life is the best religion.

Ashley Montagu
Princeton, New Jersey

Preface

I n a few years now, Christendom will celebrate two thousand years of faith in the appearance of Christ, believed to be a man-god who walked the earth and who later became the focal point for a broad range of religious beliefs called Christianity.

The anniversary date brings with it, however, a great deal of uncertainty about many core religious beliefs—Christian and non-Christian—based on the findings of scientific studies in recent years. Many scholars no longer believe in the miracles associated with religion, others challenge the accuracy of holy books, and still others are struck with the resemblance of cherished religious beliefs to the myths of primitive cultures. Even the concept of a man-god has been called into question, based in part on the prevalence of man-gods in ancient times when, as a matter of course, it appeared that the founder of a religion was designated a man-god by his followers.

This book traces the origins of such religious beliefs, most of which began thousands of years ago in very ancient civilizations or even prehistoric times. Religion is apt to consider the antiquity of the beliefs as evidence of their validity (and viability) and honor them as reflecting the wisdom of the ages. Science, on the other hand, is more apt to question the intellectual sophistication of a society that existed ten thousand years ago, or more, and characterize the ancient beliefs as fanciful or uninformed.

The debate over religious origins goes deeper still, however. Religion has held that the source of its beliefs, in the first instance, were the truths passed down from god to prophet and secured in holy writ. Science suggests that many religious beliefs are mythical in nature, coming from, and common to, the most ancient civilizations.

While the debate about a spirit world continues, it is fair to say that most of our lives have been influenced, if not defined, by a belief that unseen spirits attend us at birth, protect us from harm, provide us with food and, agreeable spirits that they are, accompany us through life on our way to a Paradise beyond. These very reassuring sequences are forfeit, of course, if there is no spirit world and our Christian beliefs were simply taken from more ancient cultures which shared our own propensity for wishful thinking.

Over fifty years ago, Sigmund Freud concluded that belief in a spirit world was, indeed, mere wishful thinking, and today most scientists would share the conclusion as stated in his *Civilization and Its Discontents*:

> I was concerned much less with the deepest sources of the religious feeling than with what the common man understands by his religion—with the system of doctrines and promises which on the one hand explains to him the riddles of this world with enviable completeness, and, on the other, assures him that a careful Providence will watch over his life and will compensate

him in a future existence for any frustrations he suffers here. The common man cannot imagine this Providence otherwise than in the figure of an enormously exalted father. Only such a being can understand the needs of the children of men and be softened by their prayers and placated by the signs of their remorse. The whole thing is so patently infantile, so foreign to reality, that to anyone with a friendly attitude to humanity it is painful to think that the great majority of mortals will never be able to rise above this view of life.[1]

The purpose of this book is to set forth the origins of our religious beliefs so that the reader may draw his or her own conclusions about the validity of Christian beliefs and those of other religions, ancient and modern. Certainly the subject matter has its fascination, for the issue at hand is how humans explain their origins and hope to relate to the world around them. And the beginning of the twenty-first century is an appropriate time, perhaps, to ponder our ancient beliefs in unseen spirits, miracles, magic spells, and other beliefs that began in preliterate times.

NOTE

1. Sigmund Freud, *Civilization and Its Discontents* (New York: W. W. Norton and Company, 1961).

1

Immortal Gods:
In the Mind of Man

here have been very few civilizations that did not worship gods. For thousands of years, most men and women have believed in powerful, albeit invisible, beings that would protect them from the onslaughts of nature and provide them with the food and shelter necessary for survival. The impulse to explain the unknown by citing unseen spirits, and the urge to enlist the help of such spirits for personal needs, has been an almost universal phenomenon.

The creation of the universe itself was once thought to have been the work of a god, or a confusion of gods, depending on the religious orientation of the observer. The Christian view of creation portrayed a greatly enlarged human being who fashioned the universe with his bare hands. Other religions have credited their gods, no less heroic in stature, with similar feats. Now, however, science rejects the idea that invisible spirits, called gods, created the universe and continue to regulate all natural phenomena.

The belief in gods began ten thousand years ago, or more, when humans had no real understanding of nature. In their innocence, they could only explain natural phenomena in terms of their own recognized abilities. They therefore assumed that rain must come from a being much like themselves, although larger and obviously invisible, who lived above the clouds and sprinkled water on the world below. Similarly, the wind arose when a very large, invisible being puffed out his cheeks and blew mighty gusts across the land. And from these innocent musings, the gods were born.

Among the more prevalent gods were those who controlled the violent weather patterns. Storms, for example, represented an awesome display of force. The sky grew dark and the wind rose to a force that could bend or break trees. Jagged shafts of light came down from a darkened sky and struck trees and huts. The effect was heightened by a tremendous booming sound which seemed to envelop the earth. The power of the storm was apparent, but an explanation for the phenomenon was not. So early humans again concluded that an unseen spirit must have caused the storm—a storm-god of threatening powers and proportions.

In other cases, the controlling spirit was thought to be smaller and friendly in nature. The movement of the human body, for example, was explained by a small spirit who resided in the body and acted as an engine of sorts. The spirit departed the body during sleep and returned during the active waking hours.

In time, every life-form and even inanimate objects were all thought to be possessed by spirits.

This idea was vividly presented by Sir James Frazer, the famous disciple of Tylor and the author of one of the most influential studies of religion, *The Golden Bough*.

> After men had peopled with a multitude of individual spirits every rock and hill, every tree and flower, every brook and river, every breeze that blew, and every cloud

that flecked with silvery white the blue expanse of heaven, they began, in virtue of what we may call the economy of thought, to limit the number of the spiritual beings of whom their imagination at first had been so prodigal. Instead of a separate spirit for every individual tree, they came to conceive of a god of the woods in general, a Silvanus or what not; instead of personifying all the winds as gods, each with his distinct character and features, they imagined a single god of the winds, an Aeolus, for example.[1]

And so animals, rocks, water, trees, and other objects in nature were invested with spirits, and humankind had a comprehensive, although mistaken, explanation for the workings of the universe.

The belief that unseen spirits pervaded the natural world was called animism. It was succeeded by religion, which gave structure and sophistication to animism, but never abandoned the belief in a spirit world. Certainly Christianity did nothing to dispel a belief in spirits when it taught that the Almighty hung out the stars each night with his giant hand, set the sun on its course each day and kept in touch with an earthbound audience by means of various signs and wonders—comets, for example, were flung across the night sky to register his displeasure (although some theologians believed they were piloted across the sky by lesser spirits). And angels, the minions of the Almighty and themselves spirits, performed such duties as opening the "windows of heaven" to let the rain fall from heaven's great cistern.

So from the earliest of ages, humanity hazarded a guess that unseen spirits orchestrated the universe. The more powerful of the spirits became gods and those of evil intent became demons. But all were merely creatures of the imagination, born of a need to understand the natural world and cope with the problems of life.

Today, these traditional religious beliefs are forfeit. Science and humanity suggest that an adventuresome spirit world, once the object of our awe, should now more properly be regarded as ancient superstition. There are knowledgeable explanations for natural phenomena and the concept of gods has not proved a serviceable one.

The idea of a spirit world nevertheless has had remarkable staying power over the centuries, and while thousands of "immortal" gods have been laid to rest, a fair number have survived the centuries and the expectations of their followers. Sigmund Freud explains this by the illusory nature of religious beliefs. He noted in *The Future of an Illusion*[2] that "the characteristic of illusions is that they are derived from human wishes." In short, Freud held that the beginning (and continuing) belief in religion, in gods, was wishful thinking on the part of a beleaguered humanity. Men and women were often incapable of explaining the natural world and seemingly helpless in the face of such threatening natural phenomena as famine, flood, quake, disease, aging and eventually death. To deal with these threats they sought, wished for, supernatural powers and then found them in the person of their gods.

Freud noted that it is a "striking fact" that religion has always been exactly what people would wish it to be. And so it is that our gods offer protection from our enemies, a cure for our diseases, solace in our distress, justice now or in the hereafter, and the means to handle any misfortune that may befall us. Religion has even engaged to defeat the natural law of death with the promise of a resurrection or reincarnation. So religion indeed offers everything that one could wish for. Our wishes, then, are the origin of our religious beliefs and the source of their staying power, and the gods are merely themes of the imagination.

There is no longer any question among psychologists that gods are products of the human imagination. A 1972 survey of members of the American Psychological Association revealed that less than two percent of the membership were theists. And the psychologists are joined by other scientists, the majority of whom have long since abandoned a belief in spirits. Even fifty years ago, most scientists did not credit the existence of God, and the proportion of unbelievers has surely increased since then.

THE BELIEF IN GOD

	Believers	Doubters	Disbelievers
Physicists	38%	16%	47%
Biologists	27	13	60
Sociologists	24	9	67
Psychologists	10	12	79

Note: Percentages may not add across to 100% due to rounding.

Source: James H. Leuba, "Religious Beliefs of American Scientists," *Harper's Monthly Magazine* (August 1934).

Freud has confirmed that after the gods were born to us they were given human identities and personalities that would facilitate a relationship: In *The Future of an Illusion*,[3] an associate noted Freud's conclusion that "the humanization of nature is derived from the need to put an end to man's perplexity and helplessness in the face of its dreaded forces, to get into a relation with them and finally to influence them." Clearly, every society wants gods who are manageable, and humans have always had an insight into how the gods could be coaxed into taking a responsible view of things. The Brahmin priests used human sacrifice and songs to achieve their ends, but they were prepared, if necessary, to punish recalcitrant gods and even create new ones. Our theologians tell us that the Christian god has committed in writing (the Bible) to answering the prayers of the faithful, and the Jewish faithful have traditionally been so confident of their requests that the deity is thanked in advance. When expedient, some religions have entered into a bargaining process with the gods, whereby foodstuffs and gifts were not turned over to the gods until the prayers were answered. It appears that nowhere in this world are the gods running out of control.

In fact, we are very protective of the behavior of our gods. We thank them for our good fortune but rarely blame them for our misfortune, not wishing to suggest any culpability on their part. Instead, we blame our priests or ourselves. Or we may simply conclude that our gods work in mysterious ways which are beyond our immediate understanding but, we like to think, have our best interests at heart in the longer term.

The humanization of the gods was taken to the next level when they were given an even more specific persona—they became father figures. Freud observed that the mother is the first to satisfy a child's need for love and to offer protection from anxieties. But then, "In this function (protection) the mother is soon replaced by the stronger father, who retains that position for the rest of childhood."[4] Our fathers, then, become the role models for our gods, who are called on to perform the same functions as human fathers, but on a grander scale.

Freud's *Future of an Illusion,* sums up the origin of religious ideas, and of gods, in these words:

> the psychical origin of religious ideas. These, which are given out as teachings, are not precipitates of experience or end results of thinking: they are illusions, fulfillments of the oldest, strongest and most urgent wishes of mankind. The secret of their strength lies in the strength of those wishes. As we already know, the terrifying impression of helplessness in childhood aroused the need for protection—for protection through love— which was provided by the father; and the recognition that this helplessness lasts throughout life made it necessary to cling to the existence of a father, but this time a more powerful one. Thus

the benevolent rule of a divine Providence allays our fear of the dangers of life; the establishment of a moral world-order ensures the fulfillment of the demands of justice, which have so often remained unfulfilled in human civilization; and the prolongation of earthly existence in a future life provides the local and temporal framework in which these wish-fulfillments shall take place.[5]

So Freud found that religious ideas and the creation of gods had a psychical origin and were, in essence, wishful thinking on the part of humans. In this respect science and religion have shared a common goal in that both attempt to satisfy human needs, religion through the creation of gods and science through the empowerment of humans. Clearly, science has been the more successful and humans have been empowered to the point that our current abilities would appear godlike to ancient peoples.

In his 1930 book, *Civilization and Its Discontents,* Freud noted that humans of that era had significantly improved, if not perfected, their motor and sensory organs. Powerful engines had increased their muscularity and placed giant forces at their disposal. Spectacles, telescopes, and microscopes had improved their vision and extended its limits. Telephones and other auditory devices had improved their hearing and extended its range across continents. Cameras and auditory recording devices had given them powers of recollection that went well beyond the human memory. These assets were cultural acquisitions, not related to religion, and yet gave to humans many powers that once were sought from their gods:

All these assets he may lay claim to as his cultural acquisition. Long ago he formed an ideal conception of omnipotence and omniscience which he embodied in his gods. To these gods he attributed everything that seemed unattainable to his wishes, or that was forbidden to him. One may say, therefore, that these gods were cultural ideals. Today he has come very close to the attainment of his ideal, he has almost become a god himself. Only, it is true, in the fashion in which ideals are usually attained according to the general judgment of humanity. Not completely; in some respects not at all, in others only half way. Man has, as it were, become a kind of prosthetic God. When he puts on all his auxiliary organs he is truly magnificent; but those organs have not grown on to him and they still give him much trouble at times. Nevertheless, he is entitled to console himself with the thought that this development will not come to an end precisely with the year 1930 A.D. Future ages will bring with them new and probably unimaginably great advances in this field of civilization and will increase man's likeness to God still more.[6]

No doubt our civilization's new use of computers to supplement human brain power, television to enhance human communications, and our recent travel in space would qualify as advances which make humans more godlike. Television, in effect, gives a spokesperson the ability to be everywhere in the world at the same time, an ability once associated only with gods (or those saints who were favored with the gift of ubiquity). Interplanetary travel was once the province of angels, whose feathered wings and flappings may now appear to be antiquated modes of flight.

So human wishes are now being satisfied by science, by human endeavor, and a greater understanding of human needs, and as a result the ancient gods are not being called on as before. Mental and physical illnesses, for example, were once the responsibility of the gods (the causes and cures), to the extent that the priesthood, Christian and others, forbade the practice of medicine as an unseemly interference with a divine prerogative. Today both priest and lay person rely on medical science to treat their mental and physical problems, and few believe that diseases which are beyond our current reach, such as AIDS, will be cured by an appeal to unseen spirits.

Humanity, therefore, which in earlier ages created gods as a way to fulfill its urgent desires, now seeks fulfillment from science, a very human resource. Human wishes have shown themselves to be a powerful force, then, strong enough to create a system of gods which has never appealed to reason, but strong enough, also, to create a more viable alternative called science which is now displacing the gods. So the origin of gods, and now their twilight, have both been brought about by the power of human wishes. And the transition from religion to science is now underway.

NOTE

1. Quoted in Richard Cavendish, *Man, Myth and Magic* (New York: Marshall Cavendish Corporation, 1983), p. 132.

2. Sigmund Freud, *The Future of an Illusion* (New York: W. W. Norton and Company, 1961), p. 31.

3. Ibid., p. 22.

4. Ibid., p. 24.

5. Ibid., p. 30.

6. Sigmund Freud, *Civilization and Its Discontents* (New York: W. W. Norton and Company, 1961), p. 38.

2

Gods of the World:
An Overview

here is ample evidence that the invention of gods and spirits resulted from the need of human beings to understand and then control the natural world as they struggled to survive.

And if one were to doubt that gods were only flights of fancy, the wondrous array of beings who achieved godhood might help to make the case. In various configurations, gods were on hand to satisfy every possible need. There was a sun-god to assure light, warmth, and energy. A rain-god to provide water. A fertility-god to assure reproduction. A thunder-god to protect against storms. A corn-goddess to assure an abundant harvest. A war-god to bring victory over the enemy. And after the basics of survival were covered, other gods and spirits were added by choice or chance; these secondary gods often dealt with indulgences such as wine, dancing, or even learning.

Geography also influenced the invention of gods. In warmer climates a sun-god was always present, and in tropical climates a rain-god. Storm-gods were pervasive, reflecting the fact that inclement weather affected every part of the globe. In heavily forested areas such as northern Europe, people worshiped trees. In elevated areas, people worshiped mountains as the abodes of gods, and coastal areas were certain to have a sea-god.

Few, if any, of the ancient gods were universal. Most were confined to very specific areas and owed their loyalties to the people of that area. An ancient Hebrew traveler might take along an oxcart of Hebrew dirt to assure that his god accompanied him on the trip. Individual cities often had their own gods, perhaps with a number of lesser spirits protecting the outlying hills and valleys. In Babylon, under Nebuchadnezzar, the assortment of gods became so burdensome that some priests tried to reduce their number and diversity by suggesting that all gods were simply different aspects of the same god, Marduk. It was hoped that this would result in a more orderly system of worship. Egypt and other lands also tried to consolidate their deities on occasion, although their attempts were often thwarted by competing priesthoods who had a personal stake in the proceedings.

Once the ancient world decided that invisible spirits controlled their destinies, they were left with the task of visualizing them. In some cases prophets reported seeing their god and were then able to describe the apparition. Otherwise, priests and shamans could decide on the appearance of their god and, given its invisible nature, they enjoyed considerable latitude.

As a result, many distinctive designs appeared. Quite a number of the ancient gods were beast-gods who possessed a combination of human and animal features, a carryover from the animal totems of earlier times. The origin of totems has been variously explained by scholars, including Freud's hypothesis that "the totem may have been the first form of the father substitute and the god a later one in which the father regained his human form."[1] If the origin of the totem was uncertain, the gods nevertheless appeared with the features of animals which were endemic to the area and often with their characteristic speed, strength, or cunning. So crocodile-gods were found in tropic waters, elephant-gods in India, buffalo-gods in the Great Plains, dolphin-gods on the coast of Brazil, bear-gods in the frozen north, and jaguar-gods in Central and South America.

The gods were often given extra arms, legs, or heads to symbolize their superhuman powers. In Hindu art the power of a god was indicated by extra arms and his divine wisdom by a third eye in the center of the forehead. Some early Christians portrayed their god as three-headed and the Christian seraph was characterized by six wings which were covered with eyes. Among the ancient Germanic peoples the god Thor was depicted as a great giant, and many Slavic gods had several heads, some facing forward and, as a precaution, some facing backward. The god Rugievit had only one head but seven faces—and seven swords hanging from his belt. The gods of Mount Olympus, called the Homeric gods, were human in appearance, but with the marvelous ability to change their size or shape at will, and they were also ageless and immortal, courtesy of the Greek author Homer, who was the first person to describe these gods to an interested Greek audience.

When the reproductive powers of a god were to be represented, many religions met the issue head on. The predecessors of the Celts used symbols of the stag or an antlered god with phallus erect, called the Horned One. As the god of reproduction, the Indian god Shiva has as his symbol the phallus which maintains a state of erection at all times. Other religions also celebrated their fertility gods with representations of a phallus, such as the Egyptian god Osiris and the Greek god Dionysus, whose phallus was prominently displayed in orgiastic rites. And as extra heads were used to symbolize the great intelligence of the gods, generous proportions were often used to symbolize the great reproductive powers of the gods.

Early Goddess

When a goddess is represented as the creator, her own body may
then become the universe.

Illustration from *Atalanta Fugiens* by Michael Maier, 1618; courtesy August C.
Long Health Sciences Library, Columbia University, New York City.

The humanization of the gods was apparent in every culture.
When given a human nature, the gods were easier to understand
and more predictable in their behavior. Thus in many parts of the
world statues of the gods were washed, clothed, and fed on a daily
basis, as if they were human. The gods were also known to dance,

love, marry, quarrel, and sometimes overindulge in food and drink. And many cultures saw the gods as a family with the father at the head, a mother figure, and children.

Sir James Frazer in his classic work *The Golden Bough* notes that the high gods of Babylon appeared to their worshipers only in dreams and visions, but they were generally believed to have human forms and emotions and were certainly human in their fate. Babylonian gods "were born into the world, and like men they loved and fought and died."

The Greek gods, too, were human in both appearance and personality. For the most part, they represented ideals of physical beauty, and although they could be angered, they were generally amiable gods. People were comfortable with an image of gods who ate and drank and shared the same amusements as they themselves did. It was even possible to laugh at the gods. Edith Hamilton cites the example, at the time, of people laughing at Zeus trying to conceal his love affairs with other women but inevitably being caught by his wife, Hera.

In India the gods represent the dual or complex nature of humans. Shiva, for example, is the destroyer but also the creator. In the Trimurti, good is mixed with evil, a warlike nature with a peaceful side, and an extreme sexual drive with a disposition to be chaste. This duality or plurality of natures does make it easier for worshipers to relate to the deity, for human nature also has its many sides.

Of course, humanization is apparent in ancestor worship. Ancestor worship probably began from the respect or authority accorded to parents and grandparents while they were alive. After their death, their survivors may have had dreams of the departed and interpreted these dreams as seeing or hearing from the dead. On occasion, the departed had gained such stature while alive that, in addition to the immediate family, the tribe or clan would worship their spirit and they would achieve the status of gods.

Ancestor worship was practiced by such diverse cultures as those of the American Indian, the ancient Inca, and the ancient Hebrew, although perhaps nowhere in the world is there such a regard and concern for the dead as in China and Japan, where ancestor worship is still an important part of religious beliefs. Ancestor worship is frequently found among many African societies as well:

> Africans believe that departed members of the family exist in a spirit world and yet maintain an interest in the lives of those who continue to live. They are regarded as a great cloud of witnesses who watch the spectacle of life. More important, the dead are believed to be able to interfere in the affairs of the living. They can help a person, a family, or an entire nation if they wish. Therefore ancestors are often consulted before a battle, before an agricultural season, or before the birth of a child.[2]

The thrust of ancestor worship in Africa, however, is not that of respect and reverence so much as awe and fear. In spite of offerings and prayers, ancestors are believed to be very capricious and often the cause of natural disasters such as droughts, famines, earthquakes, and even sickness and death. So it is the spirits of ancestors more than those of nature who enforce the ethics and values of the tribe.

Many early peoples believed that their deceased ancestors became demons, driven by their anger at dying and their envy of those who survived them. As a result the living members of the family felt hostility toward the deceased. Freud acknowledges these factors and adds to them the ambivalence of human emotions. An intense love for the departed may be mixed with feelings of hostility, for the greater part unconscious. The hostility may have been fed by memories of harshness, domination, injustice, or even imaginary slights. And so the survivor feels both grief and yet some guilty satisfaction on the death of the loved one. The survivor defends against his or her unseemly feelings by projecting the hostility to the deceased, at which point the deceased is deemed hostile—an inversion of sorts.[3]

So the gods were made in the image of humans—often from the standpoint of appearance, always from the standpoint of personality—and they were usually identifiable as father figures. Moreover, the gods were fashioned for local consumption. Black people worshiped gods with dark complexions; oriental people had gods with golden skins; white people worshiped pale gods with oval eyes.

The ancient gods, then, were representations of the culture in question. A Jewish god was Semitic in appearance (although invisible), spoke Hebrew, dressed in the fashion, lived in the area and was strongly disposed to favor the Israelites in matters involving other tribes or cultures. The Egyptian people had the same relationship with Egyptian gods. In fact, nowhere in the world were there gods who did not speak the language, follow the customs, enjoy the food and dress in the fashion of their constituency—over and above their clear disposition to favor their own kind in any controversy. Clearly, people around the world created gods in accordance with their own needs and consistent with their own cultural settings.

THE GODS OF ANCIENT EGYPT

Ancient Egypt provides an interesting example of the nature and diversity of ancient deities and their relationship with a culture. Egypt was a civilization in the lower Nile Valley that existed from about 3100 B.C.E. until the Romans occupied Egypt in 30 B.C.E.

The gods of Egypt were numerous and seemed to live together in relative harmony despite their different roles. Sebek, the personification of evil and death, coexisted with Thoth, god of learning and wisdom and the inventor of writing. As in other ancient civilizations, there was a god for every purpose.

Many of the Egyptian gods were representatives of natural forces. Re was the sun-god, Khnum the god of the Upper Nile, Seth the storm-god, Osiris the god of fertility and negotiation. Gods assured the propagation of the species, gods were on hand at the time of death, and gods were in the afterlife to protect the tombs and cemeteries. The creation of humankind, itself, was assigned to one or more gods.

The gods were also identified with cities. In *Eerdman's Handbook to the World's Religions* it notes that just as ancient Hebrew tribes each had a god, so did the Egyptian cities. Travelers from one city to another would pray to the local god, and also to any god along the way that was able to assist the traveler.

The ancient gods took bizarre forms, half animal and half human. Horus, the sky-god, had the head of a hawk. Anubis, god of the dead, had the head of a jackal. Isis, the great goddess of motherhood and fertility was sometimes represented as cow-headed. Thoth had the head of an ibis, Khnum the head of a ram. Animals were not only part of the representation of the gods, but were often considered sacred in their own right. Practices differed over the three-thousand-year history of ancient Egypt, but at one time all of the animals of a given species might be considered sacred—crocodiles, baboons, serpents. At other times a single animal, such as a bull with special marks, would be singled out for worship as the incarnation of a god. Tombs include many animals who were mummified and buried with honor.

In personality, the gods were thought to possess human traits. According to *Eerdman's Handbook to the World's Religions*:

> Egyptians thought of their gods as having the same needs and instincts as themselves. The day began with a ritual in which the god was awakened by a choir. The night attire was then removed

from the image of the god, which was washed, dressed and offered food and drink. After this the god might be called on to receive visitors, deliver oracles, or undertake some other duties. We may assume that his behavior and decisions would reflect the views and wishes of the priests who could claim to interpret them on his behalf. He would receive offerings of food during the day and eventually be put to bed for the night in his shrine.[4]

The gods would also be taken on boat trips to visit their women friends or another god. On such outings people would line the way to cheer and wave as the god's likeness passed by.

The Egyptian kings or pharaohs were also thought to be divine, although their powers were limited. As mortals, they lacked the ability to control events to the extent of the immortal gods. Kings acted both as gods and as priests to the gods, which some authorities note as one of the contradictory aspects of Egyptian religion. Frazer describes how, in ancient Egypt, "the king, as the representative of the sun, walked solemnly round the walls of a temple in order to ensure that the sun should perform his daily journey round the sky without the interruption of an eclipse or other mishap."[5]

During his seventeen-year reign, Pharaoh Amenhotep IV attempted to impose a form of monotheism on Egypt with the worship of Aton, the sun-god. Other gods were discredited and their temples destroyed, but after the pharaoh's death the power of the priests was great enough to return Egypt to its belief in many different gods.

The gods of ancient Egypt, then, were born of a desire to control the powerful forces of nature. The mysteries of birth, death, and the hope for an afterlife were each represented in the person of a god. And over its three-thousand-year history Egypt worshiped beast gods, human gods, and practiced a form of monotheism. Many of the ancient religious beliefs will be seen to have influenced other religions, including the so-called living religions.

Throughout the world, then, the invention of gods by the ancients was merely a reflection of the needs which they, as individuals and as a society, perceived as necessary for survival. If a god was fierce and warlike it was because his people felt threatened by warlike neighbors. When the Greeks portrayed their gods as frolicsome, it was a commentary on their own lifestyle—and perhaps a justification. As all gods were usually described as immortal, it betrayed a longing on the part of humans to live forever. So the gods of old were made in the image of humans and given the powers that humans wished to possess. And the gods were fashioned from local clay, shaped by the culture, the environs, and even the wildlife in given parts of the globe.

Most of the ancient gods have departed the scene by now, their vaunted immortality notwithstanding. Some were simply casualties in a highly competitive and overcrowded field. Some fell to the sword as conquering armies were accompanied by their own gods. And some gods evolved and changed identities to accommodate the needs of a government or priesthood or culture. Nevertheless, old gods do not die easily, and a number have survived for thousands of years and are still with us today. They are the gods of our living religions.

NOTES

1. Sigmund Freud, *Totem and Taboo* (New York: Vintage Books, 1946), p. 191.

2. Lewis M. Hopfe, *Religions of the World* (New York: Macmillan Publishing Co., 1987), p. 64.

3. Freud, *Totem and Taboo*, p. 79.

4. *Eerdman's Handbook to the World's Religions* (Grand Rapids: William B. Eerdmans Publishing Co., 1982).

5. Sir James G. Frazer, *The Golden Bough*, abridged ed. (New York: Macmillan Publishing Co., 1922), p. 90.

3

The Living Gods:
Western

The gods of living religions differ little from the gods worshiped by the ancient religions. They remain invisible beings whose original nature and presumed powers were revealed to a prophet. So the evidence for the existence of a particular god has been the testimony of a religious prophet who, by his or her account, sought and received a vision from the god in question.

Expectedly, the gods of today in appearance and personality are quite attuned to their constituencies and their powers are precisely those required to satisfy the needs of the individuals and societies they serve. It is certainly more than a coincidence that the gods of the world are so well suited to the times.

There are, of course, many characteristics that today's gods have in common with each other and the gods of yesteryear. The first is that they are invisible and have chosen to reveal themselves only to their prophets. Then, they are immortal and should misfortune befall them they are capable of a renewed existence. They are all-powerful and yet continue to allow the existence of good and evil. They are capricious in that human needs are responded to occasionally, but not consistently. They nevertheless demand homage and in return promise the faithful blessings in this life and bliss in an afterlife. Thus has it always been with gods, in every country and every age, and today's gods possess the very same characteristics.

Beast-gods are still with us today as they have been for thousands of years. Today, the Christian reveres angels, figures with the body of a human but the wings of a bird—and it was an angel who revealed the contents of the Quran to Muhammad. The Hindu worships the elephant-god Ganapati, among the many beast-gods in the Indian pantheon.

And we observe that the gods of one religion are occasionally handed down to another. Yahweh originated with the Hebrews but was later adopted by the Muslims. In other cases the gods were merged or absorbed, just as Buddhism accommodated many Shinto gods when it spread into Japan. Similarly, Hinduism was able to absorb many Buddhists when it described Gautama as an avatar, or incarnation, of Vishnu.

The living gods, then, show evidence of adapting to the needs of the time, which perhaps is the explanation for their longevity. As the religious prophets of the world gave birth to a particular god, the priesthood has managed to tailor the god to the occasion. The gods evolve, then, and their identities are shaped by the emotional needs of the people, the political needs of the country, and the institutional needs of the religion.

JUDAISM

The earliest form of Judaism was naturism, the belief that natural objects such as trees, stones, and mountains possessed magical powers and that unseen spirits roam the natural world. In this respect the early Hebrew religion was entirely typical of other early religions.

The Hebrew god, Yahweh, was the end result of an evolutionary process that began with naturism. T. James Meek, the author of *Hebrew Origins,* describes it this way:

> The world was full of spirits controlling and directing human affairs. Some were inherent in natural phenomena; others were the spirits of the departed. Some of the outstanding of both classes rose eventually to the rank of gods, and were given personal names; and as tribes developed, each tribe, through accident or design, hit upon some one deity to be its particular tribal god. It was as such apparently that the god Yahweh first appears on the pages of the Old Testament.[1]

The prophet Moses, of course, was credited with the selection of Yahweh as the tribal god. In presenting Yahweh to the Hebrews, Moses did not suggest that he was the only god, rather that he was the god most deserving of worship by the Hebrews. One of the considerations, certainly, was the presumed power of Yahweh relative to other gods. And from this perspective Yahweh was a logical choice, for he was recognized as a powerful volcano-god and, some believe, a powerful storm-god as well.

T. James Meek believes that Yahweh was originally a storm-god, one of several nature gods that were worshiped in earlier times. His voice was the thunderpeal and he was known as "The Rider of the Clouds." His identity as a storm-god is consistent with the powers that he was said to have exercised on behalf of the Hebrews, wherein he directed some of nature's most dreaded forces against their enemies. Scriptures say that the Red Sea was parted by winds, the Canaanites overwhelmed by a storm, the Philistines were confounded by thunder, and Israel's foes at Beth-horon were slain with hailstones. But Yahweh was also said to be connected with earthquakes and volcanic eruptions.

Freud, in *Moses and Monotheism*, identified Yahweh as "certainly a volcano-god" who at the time was thought to be "an uncanny, bloodthirsty demon who walks by night and shuns the light of day." Either as a volcano-god, or in his role as a storm-god, it is clear that Yahweh was selected for his warlike nature and ability to protect the Hebrew people. As time went on, Yahweh lost both his identity as a volcano-god and his reputation as a bloodthirsty demon, through transformations in the biblical text.

There is general agreement on the bloodthirsty nature of Yahweh, but opinions differ on other aspects of his selection. A number of modern historians, and Freud cites Eduard Meyer as one source, believe that Yahweh was chosen after the Exodus from Egypt, not before, which calls into question the Biblical account which described a series of miracles that enabled the Jews to leave Egypt. Freud contends that "No historian can regard the Biblical account of Moses and the Exodus as other than a pious myth."[2]

At whatever point Yahweh was chosen as a tribal god, he later became god of a confederacy of tribes and eventually the national god of the Hebrews. Even then, however, Yahweh was regarded as one god among many and not as a universal god; Yahweh was god of the Hebrews, just as Re was the national god of Egypt, Marduk the god of Babylonia, and Ashur the god of Assyria.

And although Yahweh was recognized as the national god, David's son Solomon still built temples to other gods, including a bull-god. Scripture mentions the "temple of the golden cow" and altars to a bull-god where the Asherah, or sacred pole, of the fertility cult could be found. Baal, whose symbol was the bull, maintained a strong hold on the Hebrews for centuries after Moses, and at times it appeared that Baal was the dominant deity and Yahweh a secondary tribal god. The closeness of the cults was apparent in that for some time the bovine became the symbol for Yahweh.

Another cult that coexisted with the Yahweh cult featured a serpent. In this case, Israelites offered sacrifices to a bronze serpent that was said to have been made by Moses himself. Reverence for the serpent continued until King Hezekiah broke the idol several centuries later.

It was the Hebrew prophets who turned the people toward the worship of one god. In *Hebrew Origins* the prophets were described as being as "jealous as they were zealous" and certainly responsible for the development of monotheism: "The Hebrew prophets began as prophets of Yahweh. That led them to oppose all alien cults, and bit by bit that led them to the position that Yahweh alone was God. With them monolatry blossomed into monotheism, nationalism into universalism. . . ."[3]

Measuring from the era of the biblical Patriarchs in 2000–1750 B.C.E., and the Exodus from Egypt led by Moses around 1200 B.C.E., it was not until the fifth century B.C.E. that the idea of monotheism was firmly established with the Hebrews. It was a time when imperialism was gaining strength—and it has been said that "monotheism is but imperialism in religion."[4]

Monotheism first appeared in Egypt during the reign of Amenhotep IV, who ascended the throne in 1375 B.C.E. Freud noted that it was "the first case in the history of mankind, and perhaps the purest, of a monotheistic religion." It was not to last, for after the pharaoh's death his Aton (a sun-god) religion was abolished, but it established the idea of one god, a universal god, who was not limited to one nation or ethnic group. Freud sees in the Aton religion the possible source of the later Hebrew belief in monotheism, although this transfer is not certain.

Although Judaism became monotheistic, it still shared with other major religions elements of mysticism. Hopfe in *Religions of the World* notes:

Jewish mysticism is as old as Judaism. Elements of the occult in Judaism have been found in the Bible, in the Talmud, and in the writing of many of its leading figures. The concern for angels, demons, magical incantations, charms, witches, ghouls, interpretation of dreams, the date of the coming of the Messiah, and the name of God have been lumped together under the heading of Cabala (tradition).[5]

Judaism emerged, then, in an early culture whose members adopted Yahweh, a volcano-god, as their own. After being chosen as a tribal god, Yahweh became god of a confederation of tribes and then the national god of the Hebrew people. Even then, there was active competition from a bull-god and a serpent cult and no claim of universality was made for Yahweh—a Hebrew god was thought to live only in the land of the Hebrews.

Over the centuries, Yahweh lost his identification as a volcano-god, and his warlike nature, and became a personal god with the appearance, thoughts, and emotions of the people who worshiped him. Later still, his universality was established through the efforts of the Hebrew prophets.

Ultimately, the Christian and Islamic religions chose him as their universal god—and the evolution from a tribal volcano-god was substantially complete. Today, from his beginnings as a volcano-god Yahweh has become what some have called a sublime abstraction.

CHRISTIANITY

Christianity began as a sect of Judaism and thus worshiped the Hebrew god, Yahweh, as its ruling spirit. It was a propitious time, as traditional religious commitments had weakened. The Roman gods were still worshiped, but not with the conviction of earlier times, and this had led to the emergence of new religious cults from Egypt, Persia, and Greece. The gods Osiris from Egypt, Mithra from Persia, and Dionysus from Greece all made inroads at

Threefold God

The Christian godhead is depicted with three heads, representing the Father, Son, and Holy Spirit.

The Library of St. John's College, Cambridge, England. Thirteenth-century English. Special collections.

this time. As a group they have been called the "mystery religions," and they shared a number of beliefs, including the promise of an eternal life, that became the central beliefs of Christianity, as well. Hopfe in *Religions of the World* characterized the mystery religions as common in these respects:

> Each offered the believer life after death in one form or another. Many had secret rituals to which only the initiated were invited. Many had sacred communion meals and baptisms that aided the participant in the search for eternal life. Most of the mystery religions accepted people into these groups without regard to race or social status. In the homogenized life of the Roman Empire, when a large portion of the population was made up of slaves, this was an important feature indeed.[6]

Among the milieu of mystery religions, Christianity prevailed and became the official religion in the Roman Empire, after which there could be no further challenges from other gods. Yahweh, however, continued to evolve in keeping with his new role. The God of the Old Testament had been fierce and full of vengeance, as befit a god whose duty was to protect the Hebrew people. The God of the New Testament, written from 51 to 95 C.E., was milder, more merciful, and with a universal appeal which fit in well with the missionary work the Christians were undertaking throughout the Roman Empire.

Christian belief has continued to evolve through the years and worshipers now believe in one God who is a Trinity consisting of the Father, Son, and Holy Spirit. This concept of God as One Being in three persons serves to differentiate Christianity from Judaism and Islam, yet all are said to be monotheistic.

Although monotheism has served to limit the number of gods, it has not always limited the number of other spirits associated with a religion. From the beginning, Christianity offered the faithful a full complement of demigods, angels, and ghosts, who would work in association with their God. Then there were devils, dragons, and an array of creatures from the underworld who would work in opposition. These auxiliary beings offered benefits to both the worshiper and the religion: the benevolent spirits gave added protection to the worshiper and offered attractive images; the malevolent spirits explained the existence of evil and underscored the need for divine protection. Together, the collection of spirits represented a comprehensive presentation of the religious idea, and one charged with drama.

Christianity, then, worshiped the Hebrew god, Yahweh, as its ruling spirit. And from the Hebrews, and other ancient religions, it adopted a number of auxiliary figures. The idea of Satan is thought to have come from the ancient Persian prophet, Zoroaster, who also contributed the idea of angels, although the appearance of the Christian angel was derived from the Greek Goddess of Victory, Nike.

The winged Nike was an apt choice for the prototype of angels, as their most important function is said to involve bringing messages from God to man. They may also intervene in human affairs and destroy or punish, help or save. At death, angels are said to come and lead the souls of the deceased into the next world. Saint Augustine thought that the procreation of living creatures, including humans, could not be explained except by the participation of angels. They were not necessarily creators of life, but were helpers in a manner that humans were not capable of discerning.

One knows that angels exist, Saint Augustine once said, through faith. The *New Catholic Encyclopedia* talks of the modern attitude toward a belief in angels:

> In the modern mind angels are considered to be tenuous creatures who, with the passage of time, are more and more being relegated to the sphere of legend, fairy tale and child's fancy. Then, of course, there was rationalism, which thought that all

belief in the existence of angels should be repudiated. Inasmuch as they are considered to be products of the imagination, their existence is widely denied. The believing Christian, however, will even today maintain that there are angels because the Bible and the church teach it.[7]

The entourage of angels and other spirits that follow the Christian God may also reflect the fact that worshipers find an "almighty" god remote and difficult to identify with. A corn-goddess can be portrayed with yellow tresses and her bounty consumed daily, or a wine-god can easily be imagined in an attitude of revelry, but an "almighty" god is seldom seen in a down-to-earth situation, as it were. So other spirits are personified and satisfy a desire for something which, if not tangible, is at least familiar and imaginable. The adoration of saints may be another reflection of this need.

Devotion to saints began only as a form of honor and imitation of their virtue, but by the third century Christians believed that saints could intercede with God on their behalf. The importance of saints grew through the centuries as their lives were publicized, churches placed under their patronage, and their remains (relics of feet, hands, hair, bodily parts) venerated. The *New Catholic Encyclopedia* notes that: "Though the early theologians carefully distinguished between honor of the saints and adoration of God, there were at first no suitable terms to express the distinction." Exaggerated devotion to the saints brought protests from the church in the twelfth century and from the thirteenth to sixteenth centuries various Protestant leaders such as Luther, Zwingli, and Calvin rejected the invocation and intercession of the souls of departed saints, although Roman Catholics still believe in the power of saints.

Christianity, then, was heir to the god of the Hebrews, and from a number of ancient religions brought forth an impressive array of good and evil spirits and the concept of a man-god. Beyond the personages, most of the attendant Christian beliefs were from ancient stock as well, some reaching back to prehistoric times. In the main, of course, the same may be said of other living religions.

ISLAM

Before Islam, the Arab people believed in a single, all-powerful god they called Allah, which means "the God." Allah was a remote god, however, and most of the people worshiped their local and tribal gods; there were also angels and fairies to help in the struggle, and demonic creatures called jinn. The pre-Islamic religion was basically animistic, wherein spirits were believed to reside in rocks, trees, water, and all of nature.

The prophet Muhammad unified the Arab people in 630 C.E. after a series of armed conflicts with the Meccans and Jews of the area. In the end, Muhammad entered Mecca with a force of ten thousand men and destroyed the idols and images in the Kaaba. From this point on Muhammad became the leader of the Arabian people and his religious beliefs were to prevail.

The Muslims now believe in only one God, who is called Allah, and who, presumably, is the same God worshiped by Christians and Jews. Of all the other great religions of the world, only the Jewish religion believes as firmly in one God, complete and undivided.

Although Allah is alone as the god figure in Islam, he is nevertheless surrounded by other forms for good and evil. There are, for example, flights of angels to do his bidding and who act as warriors in battles against the infidels. The angel Gabriel was said to have revealed their sacred book, the Quran, to Muhammad. And there are creatures called jinn, created by fire, who are halfway between humans and angels. Some are helpful creatures who act as guardian angels; others are demons led by their leader Iblis, who is a fallen angel. Iblis is very much a Satan figure and according to Muslim legend was responsible for the fall of Adam.

Muhammad is believed to be the last and greatest of the prophets, who included Abraham, Moses, and Jesus. In his lifetime, Muhammad never claimed to be divine. And so: "There is no God but Allah; Muhammad is the messenger of Allah" (The Shahadah).

Overall, the gods of most religions have undergone a transformation in keeping with the culture, which finally has found it easier to accept evolutionary change than to create all-new gods. Such a transformation was necessary lest the god appear incongruous in appearance or personality as the society advances in sophistication. A buffalo-god, for example, would strike a dissonant note in contemporary America, although there was a time when they were commonplace.

Perhaps the most striking example of evolutionary change has been in Yahweh, who began as a tribal god of the Hebrews and went on to become a universal god worshiped by Christians, Jews, and Muslims, and who evolved over the centuries from a fierce volcano-god to what has become an abstraction in our times.

Yahweh's evolution probably reflects the central tendency for gods to become less vivid in their portrayal as time passes, which eases the way for their evolution and also gives them a broader, more universal appeal. As the gods become less distinct, however, they become less real in the minds of the faithful and less of a vital force. The god, or religion, becomes more of an ethical than a religious concept. As the persona of the god Yahweh has become less distinct over the centuries, the reality of the Christian demons, witches, angels and dragons has also faded. We seldom have sightings anymore of Hecate and her train of questing spirits in the night sky. And Freud points out that where "the Mosaic religion had been a Father religion; Christianity became a Son religion. The old God, the Father, took second place; Christ, the Son, stood in his stead."[8]

NOTES

1. T. James Meek, *Hebrew Origins* (New York: Harper and Row, 1960), pp. 91–92.

2. Sigmund Freud, *Moses and Monotheism* (New York: Vintage Books, 1967), p. 38.

3. Meek, *Hebrew Origins,* p. 225.

4. H. Breasted, *The Development of Religion and Thought in Ancient Egypt* (New York: Charles Scribner, 1912), p. 315.

5. Lewis M. Hopfe, *Religions of the World* (New York: Macmillan Publishing Co., 1987), p. 303.

6. Ibid., p. 330.

7. "Angels," *New Catholic Encyclopedia* (New York: McGraw-Hill, 1967), p. 513.

8. Freud, *Moses and Monotheism,* p. 111.

4

The Living Gods:
Eastern

*T*he gods of the East are not unlike the historical gods of the West, although there are differences in the respective religious teachings. Hinduism, for example, gives its followers license to believe in one or more gods or no gods at all. In Japan, Shinto gods coexist easily with the gods of Mahayana Buddhism. Jainism acknowledges no god and has been called an atheistic religion.

In origin, a number of the Eastern religions began more as philosophies and only later developed a religious orientation. Buddhism, for example, began with an emphasis on ethics and self-understanding rather than traditional religious beliefs. Taoism also began more as a philosophy than a religion, and Confucianism was originally concerned with human relationships and good government. In varying degrees, religious beliefs and trappings were added as time went on, in most cases after the death of the founders.

It has been true of both Eastern and Western religions that they demonstrate an ability to adapt to the needs of the times. New gods may be created, specialties among the gods may be recognized, and some of the older gods fall from favor. Historically, several of the major Eastern religions have shown a willingness to accommodate the gods of other religions, as well as the religious beliefs associated with the god, when it was to their advantage to do so.

HINDUISM

Traces of the Hindu religion may date back to the third millennium B.C.E. In the second millennium B.C.E. India was invaded by waves of Aryans whose culture and religion mingled with those of the Indian natives. The Aryans who did not migrate into India were the founders of Zoroastrianism in the area which later became the Persian Empire.

The Aryan invaders worshiped many gods but seem to have centered on nature. They worshiped the sun, moon, wind, and soil. And to placate these gods of nature they sacrificed animals and offered foodstuffs.

The Vedic books are the sacred literature of Hinduism and describe many Aryan and pre-Aryan gods. The most frequently mentioned is Indra, the god of storms and the ruler of heaven. But there is Agni, the god of fire and sacrifice; and Varuna, who can forgive sinners; and Yama, the god of the dead. This era of religion is referred to by some as Brahminism or classical Hinduism.

After classical Hinduism, the people maintained the earlier literature and the same pantheon of gods, but interest now focused on Brahman as the supreme god. Brahman is regarded as one god and undivided, but with three forms or natures called the Trimurti: Brahma, the creator; Vishnu, the preserver; and Shiva, the destroyer.

Brahma, the creator, is depicted with four bearded faces and four arms in which he holds the four Vedas. He may be seen riding on a swan or sitting on a lotus, which signifies that he is not begotten but was created by himself. His consort is the goddess Sarasvati.

Vishnu, the preserver, is a god of love and forgiveness and is thought to be in charge of human fate. He is often portrayed symbolically mounted on the heavenly eagle (garuda), or perhaps asleep on the ocean. His concern for humanity led him to make nine trips into the world in various forms (avatars)—Krishna is one incarnation, Buddha is now thought to be another. His female counterpart is Lakshmi, the symbol of beauty and good fortune.

Shiva, the destroyer, is the most popular god of the Trimurti. Shiva is the god of death and destruction and is a special god to the Indian ascetics, who may see in Shiva support for their self torment. But Shiva is also the god of dance—an embodiment of cosmic energy and reflecting the rhythms of the universe. As god of reproduction his symbol is the phallus and he maintains a state of erection at all times. A bull is frequently seen in temples as a symbol of his virility.

Shiva has many goddesses as consorts who are also very popular with the people. Kali is the most important of the consorts. She is portrayed as even more ferocious than Shiva, wearing a garland of skulls and a skirt of severed hands. On the other hand, Kali can be portrayed as peaceful and serene.

The gods of Hinduism are portrayed in many different forms, with several heads or extra arms and often with animal parts. The Greeks portrayed their gods in human form; Hindu art suggests that the gods are more powerful and important than humans by giving the gods added values. Power is indicated by extra arms. Divine wisdom may be depicted by a third eye in the center of the forehead. And animals are frequently used to show certain characteristics; for example, the god Hanuman is shown as a monkey to indicate his clever nature and agility.

One of the best-known symbols of Hinduism is the sacred cow,

A Hindu God

The Hindu religion endows gods with human or animal manifestations, sometimes both. Shown is the elephant-headed god Ganesha.

Spec-pub *Splendors of the Past,* 198a. Victor R. Boswell Jr. © National Geographic Society, Washington, D.C.

which is a living symbol of a bountiful nature. Worshipers feed the cow as an act of devotion and use its urine as a way to purify those who have broken caste, that is, have violated their hereditary social class by engaging in occupations or personal associations which are forbidden to their class. In fact, reverence for the cow is one of the more universal aspects of a religion where followers may believe in one god, many gods, or no gods at all.

BUDDHISM AND JAINISM

Hinduism gave rise to two new religions in the sixth century B.C.E.: Jainism and Buddhism. Both of the new religions rejected the sacred scriptures of Hinduism and the institutions of the caste system and sacrifice.

Jainism is of special interest because it acknowledges no creator and no supreme being. The world has always existed and there are not gods to help man in this life nor to aid in his salvation—to these ends, prayer and worship are therefore worthless because humans must rely on themselves. People are helped only by the guidelines of the Tirthankaras, the twenty-four great heroes who set examples of right conduct, faith, and knowledge. In this respect, Jainism has been called an atheistic religion.

Buddhism also began with emphasis on ethics and self-understanding rather than as a religion in the traditional sense. Buddha was not viewed either as a god or as a mediator sent by a god. He was essentially a teacher whose focus was helping people to help themselves.

Immediately after Buddha's death, however, his disciples disagreed on the true meaning of his teaching and split into two groups. The smaller and more orthodox group were the Theravada, who continued to believe that people must work out their own salvation. So, if there were gods, they were irrelevant to human destiny. The Theravada Buddhists, and a number of spinoffs, are now centered in the nations of Southeast Asia, Burma, and Sri Lanka. Lewis M. Hopfe in his book *Religions of the World* questions whether Theravada Buddhism had a broad enough appeal to become a major international religion. It was essentially a nonreligion because it called for everyone to work out their own salvation without help from the gods.

The other wing of Buddhism, called Mahayana, met the usual requirements for expansion on an international basis. The Mahayanists added new teachings and developed the idea that Buddha was, after all, divine and had come to earth to help people. They went on to suggest many other divine beings who had preceded and followed Gautama and still others who were yet to put in an appearance. The presence and possibilities of these gods established a new basis for worship and therefore priests, temples, and rituals. As Gautama was now considered only one incarnation in a series, Buddhist missionaries entered new countries and accepted the local gods as further incarnations of the Buddha. The strength of this approach made Buddhism a highly successful missionary religion and brought many more gods into the fold. Buddhism became the major religion of China and over the years spread to Korea, Japan, and other Asian nations. In India, however, Buddhism was decimated by the Muslim invasion and, by the seventh century, Hinduism had absorbed many Buddhists by describing Gautama as an avatar of Vishnu.

SIKHISM

The Sikh religion originated in recent times (about 1500) in an area of Pakistan called the Punjab. It is considered an ethnic religion because living in the area implies membership in the religion. The Sikh faith is very closely identified with the Punjab.

The religion began in the northwest area of India when Muslim invaders succeeded in establishing a strong following for the Islamic religion. There were frequent fights between the native Hindus and the Muslim converts, reflecting the essential differences in the two religions. Muslims, for example, worshiped only one true god while Hindus characteristically worshiped a pantheon of deities.

The founder of Sikhism was a man named Nanak, who was born into a Hindu home but was taught in a Muslim school. After a reported vision from God, he acted as prophet for a new religion which was to combine elements of both the Hindu and Islamic beliefs. Nanak taught the Muslim concept of one God, and the Hindu concept of reincarnation. Unlike many Indian religions, Nanak permitted his followers to eat animals on the basis that human beings were the primary creation of God. Many of the ceremonies and rituals that often surround religion were abandoned.

Nanak was considered a guru. Born in 1469, he was the first of the gurus to guide the Sikh faith. The Sikhs refer to the ten gurus as candles which have been lit from each other. The last of the ten gurus, Gobind Singh, died in 1708 but had established the Granth, or sacred scripture, as the governing principles for later generations of Sikhs. Gobind Singh also completed the change of the Sikhs from a religion of pacifism to a strong tradition of self-defense and war. The Sikhs have been involved in conflict almost from the beginning, and have been both aggressors and victims of violent neighbors.

There are two other sects within Sikhism, each presenting some variations on the central theme. The Udasis sect are essentially holy men who believe in asceticism. They are celibate, and possess only a begging bowl while going naked or wearing coarse garments. The Sahajdharis sect is not militaristic and is more conservative in outlook.

The Sikhs remain a minority group, neither Hindu nor Muslim, and religious and political hostilities continue to exist. It is an unusual combination of the mystical and military.

TAOISM

The earliest record of religious activity in China indicates a belief in many gods and the worship of ancestors. The Chinese followed a pattern that was typical of primitive societies by being both polytheistic and animistic. The mighty gods of heaven and earth were worshiped as a way to ensure good harvests. There were good spirits known as Shen and evil spirits known as Kwei, with sacrifices made to each. The ancient Chinese also attempted to predict the future through divination, with, for example, a diviner writing questions to the spirits on the shell of a turtle or shoulder blade of an ox.

Ancestral worship began in 1100 B.C.E. during the Chow dynasty and became popular in 551–479 B.C.E. when Confucius taught respect for parents and elders. In *The World's Religions* Chua Wee Hian notes:

> The Chinese believe that at death the soul of the deceased ancestor resides in three places. One part goes to heaven, the second remains in the grave to receive sacrifices and the third is localized in the ancestral tablet or shrine.[1]

Rituals address the need to provide the soul of the departed ancestor with conveniences for the next life and also to placate the evil spirits that roam the earth. Parents and grandparents are revered while living and in death may be able to help the living because of their involvement in the spirit world.

Taoism may have begun well before the sixth century B.C.E. when its founder, Lao-tzu, wrote the definitive book on Taoist beliefs. It began more as a philosophy than a religion and was concerned with respect for life, modesty in demeanor, and contempt for ambition, wealth, and pomp. There was no concern with gods or demons.

But after several centuries, Taoism began to take on mystical overtones as followers searched for ways to extend the life they so revered. Fasting, breath control, and special diets were examined as means to prolong life and possibly to achieve immortality. The art of alchemy was employed and alchemists came to believe that spirits might be involved in the process. Since alchemy was done at a stove, alchemists began to offer sacrifices to the god of the stove, Tsao Chun, who emerged as the first god of Taoism. This was in the third century C.E., and many gods were to follow.

From a philosophy that gave no consideration to a spirit world, Taoism had moved through a mystical phase and then became a religion in all respects. Gods were acknowledged and they were accompanied by priests, temples, ritual prayers, and sacrifices. Today, Taoism is a combination of the ancient Taoist philosophy and the magic and religion that evolved. Some suggest that today's educated and upper class Chinese respect the philosophical ideas of Taoism but regard the religious aspects as "fit only for the ignorant masses."

CONFUCIANISM

Confucianism began as a philosophy and has never been a religion in the traditional sense. Confucius (551–479 B.C.E.) was a teacher whose writings were concerned with ethics and human relationships. He exhibited a special interest in the principles of good government. There was no evidence of an interest in starting a religion and there was no claim that his writings were divinely inspired.

Some believe that Confucius was an agnostic and perhaps an atheist, although it is contested. At least it appears that his interest in religion was secondary to his interest in government and his faith in prayer secondary to his belief in the social order as a way of providing a good life. The nature of his beliefs is well summarized by a passage from *Religions of the World*:

> Because of the natural morality of humanity, Confucius believed that it was not necessary to offer people rewards or punishments to induce them to good conduct. Good conduct is its own reward. Therefore, whatever Confucius might have believed about the gods, he never spoke of an afterlife in heaven or hell to reward good deeds or punish evil. Under the proper conditions, people simply grow and develop into what Confucius called the "Superior Man."[2]

Thus Confucius's beliefs were quite different from those of Christianity which sees evil as the natural state of mankind—therefore requiring religion to achieve salvation. Following Confucius's death in 479 B.C.E., his principal disciple, Mencius, continued to teach the basic goodness of man. After Mencius's death another well-known interpreter, Hsun Tzu, supposed that men were basically evil in nature but maintained that proper social training, not religion, was the answer.

SHINTO

The Japanese culture is one of the youngest of the Asian nations. Very little is known about Japan's culture or religion until the fourth century C.E. The earliest forms of worship apparently centered on spirits believed to live in natural objects such as trees, mountains, and rocks and therefore would be called animist. The myths of prehistoric Japan reflect a multitude of gods, goddesses, and spirits as well as ancestor worship.

In the fifth century C.E. Japan felt the impact of other Asian cultures, particularly those of China and Korea. Japan had no written language at the time and adopted the Chinese script and other elements of the older Chinese culture. Taoism and particularly Buddhism and Confucianism were welcomed by the Japanese, who found common ground in the aspects of ancestor worship and who recognized the value of Confucian ethics in building a stable social order.

From the fifth century onward many Shinto beliefs merged with the beliefs of Mahayana Buddhism. Buddhism, according to form, altered to accommodate many Shinto gods until a wide range of different religious beliefs had developed. To many Japanese, the Shinto religion served more to guide the activities of this life while the Buddhist religion was concerned with the life to come. All of the religions lived in harmony, but the Shinto religion assumed a very secondary role.

The Tokugawa regime (1600–1867) restored the importance of Shinto in Japan. Military leaders were anxious to remove outside influences, so they pushed Buddhism and Christianity aside and supported Shinto as the state religion. During this era of militarism, the Japanese brought forth the Samurai warriors and developed the warrior code of Bushido. Japan was opened to world trade in 1854 when Commodore Perry of the United States Navy sailed into Tokyo Bay and forced the hand of the Japanese rulers. Japan began a new era of industrial growth and rewrote its constitution in 1889 to define the role of religion. The new constitution called for Shinto to be the state religion and for revival of the government's financial support, but allowed Buddhism, Christianity, and other religions to coexist.

Essentially, there are three forms of Shinto. State Shinto is the first, and it serves to encourage patriotism and loyalty to the empire of Japan. The constitution of 1889 provided that Japan would be ruled by an unbroken line of emperors and that each emperor was divine—literally a descendant of the sun-goddess Amaterasu.

Sectarian Shinto is the second form of the religion, and this may be divided into three groups. One group venerates mountains and is dedicated to asceticism, such as fire-walking, and nature worship. A second group emphasizes shamanism (predicting the future), divination (e.g., reading tea leaves), and particularly faith healing. Chanting, ecstatic dance, purification through fasting, breath control, and bathing in cold water are part of Sectarian Shinto.

The third form of Shinto is Domestic Shinto. Many Japanese houses have shrines which contain images of their patron deities. The worship may be a simple daily prayer, along with an offering of flowers, incense, or food accompanied by a ritual clapping of hands.

Still, the Japanese regard Buddhism as the religion of choice for affairs of the afterlife. Shinto is concerned with this world, Buddhism the next.

After World War II, the emperor of Japan was obliged to announce that he was not divine and the Japanese government was forbidden to support Shinto with government funds. Nevertheless, the imperial family is held in great esteem and Shinto continues to be a strong force in the political and religious life of Japan.

NOTES

1. Quoted in *Eerdman's Handbook to the World's Religions* (Grand Rapids: William B. Eerdmans Publishing Co., 1982), p. 247.

2. Lewis M. Hopfe, *Religions of the World* (New York: Macmillan Publishing Co., 1987), p. 218.

5

Human Gods:
A Religious Tradition

umans have not always stood in great awe of gods and spirits. Many peoples respected and even feared the gods but also believed that their own magic was strong enough to deal with the gods on a reasonably equitable basis. So humans believed that, through magic, they possessed godlike powers. Therefore it was not that great a step if, on a display of unusual powers, a man was promoted to the rank of man-god.

Many years ago in western India a man sought the post of incarnate human god and, assisted by a vision, won the acceptance of his fellow men. Indeed, as a reincarnation of Gunputty, the elephant-headed god, the man and his descendants were authorized to reign as gods for a period of seven generations. When the family's term of godhood had expired, the investment in church property and other considerations caused the people to find still another holy vessel, so that the spirit of Gunputty has been sustained in an unbroken line of incarnate human gods over the years.

This example of Gunputty speaks to the enterprise of individuals who aspire to the divine kingdom, the desire or even dependency of people on godlike figures, and perhaps the sheer momentum of a religious belief as it travels through the centuries.

Sir James Frazer notes many other examples of human gods. The following four examples are excerpts from *The Golden Bough*:[1]

According to the early Portuguese historian, Dos Santas, the Zimbas, or Muziambas, a people of South Eastern Africa, "do not adore idols or recognize any god, but instead they venerate and honour their king, whom they regard as a divinity, and they say he is the greatest and best in the world. And the king says of himself that he alone is god of the earth, for which reason if it rains when he does not wish it to do so, or it is hot, he shoots arrows at the sky for not obeying him." (p. 112)

*   *   *

A Hindoo sect, which has many representatives in Bombay and Central India, holds that its spiritual chiefs or Maharajas, as they are called, are representatives or even actual incarnations on earth of the god Krishna. And as Krishna looks down from heaven with most favour on such as minister to the wants of his successors and vicars on earth, a peculiar rite called Self-devotion has been instituted, whereby his faithful worshipers make over their bodies, their souls, and, what is perhaps still more important, their worldly substance to his adorable incarnations; and women are taught to believe that the highest bliss for themselves and their families is to be attained by yielding themselves to the embraces of those beings in whom the divine nature mysteriously coexists with the form and even the appetites of true humanity. (p. 116)

*   *   *

A register of all the incarnate gods of the Chinese empire is kept in the Li fan yuan or Colonial Office at Peking. The number of gods who have thus taken out a license is one hundred and sixty. Tibet is blessed with thirty of them, Northern Mongolia rejoices in nineteen, and Southern Mongolia basks in the sunshine of no less than fifty-seven. The Chinese government, with a paternal solicitude for the welfare of its subjects, forbids the gods on the register to be reborn anywhere but in Tibet. They fear lest the birth of a god in Mongolia should have serious political consequences by stirring the dormant patriotism and warlike spirit of the Mongols, who might rally round an ambitious native deity of royal lineage and seek to win for him, at the point of the sword, a temporal as well as a spiritual kingdom. (p. 119)

*   *   *

And to this day in India all living persons remarkable for great strength or valour or for supposed miraculous powers run the risk of being worshiped as gods. Thus, a sect in the Punjab worshiped a deity whom they called Nikkal Sen. This Nikkal Sen was no other than the redoubted General Nicholson, and nothing that the general could do or say damped the ardour of his adorers. The more he punished them, the greater grew the religious awe with which they worshiped him. (p. 115)

The tradition of incarnate human gods in Babylonia was well known—a long succession of rulers were deified in their lifetime. The tradition appeared to begin following the death of Sargon, who about 2800 B.C.E. founded a dynasty. (Sargon was the ruler who, as a baby, was placed in a basket of reeds and set afloat on the Euphrates, later to become the protege of the goddess Ishtar, a ruler and saint—the supposed source of the story about Moses.) Following the reign of Sargon, human gods were the rule rather than the exception:[2]

- *Rimush*, who was perhaps Sargon's immediate successor, was during his lifetime regarded as a god. What the cause was that led his subjects to accord him this honour we do not know, but it was no doubt the possession of qualities that passed among them for saintliness.

- *Naram-Sin,* of the same dynasty, whose reign of forty-four years began about 1700 B.C.E., was also regarded as a god while he lived. We know that he was a successful warrior and a great builder, but why he more than many others should have been accorded this honor we do not know.
- *Shargalisharri* was Naram-Sin's successor. His name is once preceded by the determinative for deity in one of his own inscriptions. He probably inherited the honor from his predecessor.
- *Gudea,* the great Patesi of Lagash about 2500 B.C.E., was also deified. He appears as a god in certain proper names, such as Gin-Gudea and Lu-Gudea. Probably this occurred in his lifetime, though the names in question come from the dynasty of Ur.
- *Dungi,* of the dynasty of Ur, who ruled 2429–2371 B.C.E., was the next king, so far as we know, to be deified during his lifetime.
- *Bur-Sin, Gimil-Sin,* and *Ibi-Sin,* three successors of Dungi, were also accounted divine. Their names are regularly written preceded by determinatives for deity.
- The names of other kings are at times found preceded by the determinative for deity, e.g., Ur-Ninib, Irraimiti, Zanbia, Ishbiurra, Idin-Dagan, Ishmi-Dagan, Libit-Ishtar, Itirpisha, Daniqilu-shu, Ibiq-Ada, Nur-Adad, Warad-Sin, Rim-Sin, and Hammurabi. All these were deified for the same reason.

Babylon was not the only source of a tradition which resulted in the deification of rulers and religious leaders. Whereas some of the Babylonian kings were given the status of gods, all of the Egyptian kings were so honored. *The Encyclopaedia of Religion and Ethics* notes that: "The cause that led to this is shrouded in the mystery that conceals all things prehistoric, but it was probably the primitive way of recognizing that one who could gain control over his fellows possessed rare ability. Such ability was regarded as an especial attribute of divinity. Some Egyptian kings, such as Mena, Khufu, and Thothmes III, possessed unusual ability. The divinity of many of the kings was, however, purely traditional."[3]

Throughout the pages of history, then, most of the countries of the world and many, if not most, religions have boasted an incarnate human god. We have seen several examples, but there are many:

- The early Babylonian kings claimed to be living gods and had temples built and sacrifices made in their honor.
- The kings of Egypt were deified in their lifetime and claimed divine authority over all lands and nations.
- Montezuma, the last king of Mexico, was worshiped as a god. Other Mexican kings claimed control over the weather.
- The Dalai Llama of Lhasa, Tibet, has always been regarded by his followers as a living god.
- Brahmin priests were considered to be human gods, and with the power to control the immortal gods—and if necessary, to create new ones.
- Buddha, who was not viewed as a god during his lifetime, was proclaimed a human god by the Mahayanists following his death.
- When Demetris Poliorcetes restored the Athenian democracy (307 B.C.E.), the Athenians gave divine honors to him and his father, Antigonus, both alive, under the title of the Savior Gods.

Human gods also became familiar figures in the Roman Empire—before and after the birth of Christ—with many well-known

Christ Tempted

Christ as man-god is challenged by the devil to prove His supernatural powers. Other religions have reported similar set-tos.

Church of St. Martin, Switzerland. Sonia Halliday Photographs, England.

names in evidence. For example, the Roman senate enrolled Julius Caesar among the gods after his assassination in 44 B.C.E., and some parts of the Roman Empire demanded the deification of Augustus, Caesar's successor, while he was still alive. Caligula

(12–41 C.E.) insisted on being recognized as a god while still alive. It became customary for all the emperors of Rome to receive consideration for a place among the gods (except for unsuccessful military commanders).

At the time of Christ, then, the idea of an incarnate god was not unusual. Still, the belief in Christ's divinity was not accepted by either the Jewish religious establishment or the Roman government at the time; only Christ's disciples believed that he was the Son of God. Later, after Christianity became the state religion of the Roman Empire, Christ was proclaimed the Son of God by the Roman authorities. The divinity of Christ remains a point of contention for Muslims and Jews, who recognize him as a prophet and leader, but not as an incarnate human god.

The story does not end there with respect to Christianity, however. Over the centuries many Christians believed that Christ— and God himself—was incarnate in every Christian, and these same believers therefore adored each other. In the second century Tertullian noted that this was the belief among his fellow Christians in Carthage. We are told that the disciples of Saint Columbia worshiped him as an embodiment of Christ and Sir James Frazer adds that "in the eighth century Elipandus of Toledo spoke of Christ as 'a god among gods' meaning that all believers were gods just as truly as Jesus himself."[4]

Perhaps the status of human gods has been further confused by the extraordinary powers attributed to the Christian saints. Literally thousands of Christian saints (and those of other religions) are said to have performed miracles that are godlike in every respect. If Christ exercised his powers as a human god to raise Lazarus from the dead, Saint Xavier was said by one of his biographers to have raised more than a dozen people from the dead. And various Christian saints were said to have walked on water, healed lepers, given sight to the blind, produced food miraculously—in short, to have performed all of the miracles attributed to Christ and more for good measure. To some, the result of such stories is to call into question both the miracles of Christ and the miracles of the saints—which are the basis for his godhood and their sainthood.

A belief in incarnate human gods has persisted in several parts of the world. In the year 646 the emperor of Japan was recognized as a man-god and ruler of the universe; as recently as 1889, the Japanese constitution reaffirmed his divine status. After World War II, the emperor was obliged by the United States occupation force to deny his divinity. This was an instance, then, where the divinity of their emperor had begun by proclamation and continued for over one thousand years until, by another proclamation, their belief in a man-god was suspended.

So, in the case of incarnate human gods, the aspirations of an individual and the inclinations of a people have sometimes resulted in a belief that has persisted over the centuries. Certainly it has been in the nature of a religious tradition to assign the status of human god to the founder of the religion. Or, alternatively, a prophet has been given such prestige and power as to approach godhood in the eyes of the faithful.

NOTES

1. Sir James G. Frazer, *The Golden Bough,* abridged ed. (New York: Macmillan Publishing Co., 1922).

2. James Hastings, ed., "Saints and Martyrs," *The Encyclopaedia of Religion and Ethics* (New York: Charles Scribner and Sons, 1951), p. 75.

3. Ibid.

4. Frazer, *The Golden Bough,* p. 117.

6

Prophecy:
A Word from on High

In ancient times, the status of incarnate human gods represented the highest attainment of mortal man, and was clearly the most demanding role in the religious drama. As a living god, one was expected to produce miracles for the faithful on request. The prophet, on the other hand, was believed to be possessed by a god on a temporary basis only, with an implied responsibility for passing on the words of the god but not necessarily for creating miracles.

The evidence of temporary incarnation, or possession, by a god was quite similar in most ancient societies. The prophet ordinarily showed possession by shivering, convulsing, babbling incoherently, and displaying signs that his own personality lay in abeyance—suggesting that an outside spirit had taken over. To achieve this state of spiritual promise, prophets frequently induced an ecstatic trance by physical exertion, rhythmic chants, and often the use of tobacco, alcohol, or the juice of plants with hallucinogenic properties. In many cases, epileptic seizures have been taken as signs of spiritual possession.

The basis for the ancient belief in prophecy seems clear. Divination was born of an age-old wish by humans to anticipate events and thereby gain some advantage over the fates. The desire to foretell events ranked alongside the desire for eternal life in the human hope chest, and as a result soothsayers of many persuasions arose and offered their predictions of things to come, including a life to come. Magic had offered its initiates a window on the future through astrology, numerology, tarot cards, and tossing bones. Divination through dreams was an alternative, along with an assortment of omens not at all limited to comets and falling stars. Religious prophecy was yet another way to foretell the future and reveal the secrets of the universe.

The religious prophet differed from other diviners only in that unseen spirits were said to be the source of his information, not tea leaves or telltale cloud formations. He made no claim of miraculous powers for himself, other than an ability to communicate with a spirit world and pass along their revelations. It was inevitable that the prophet, having foretold certain events, would then provide his audience with the means to deal with those events, especially when the news was not good. His suggestion was usually sacrifice or prayer, or perhaps behavior that was judged pleasing to the spirits. Since credibility required that the spirits be identified by name, together with some description of their appearance, nature and powers, the prophet was often author of the ruling spirits or gods, although the prophet also worked on occasion through a god already accepted by the faithful. As might be expected, great prestige attached to those prophets who were spokespersons for the gods.

The ancient religious prophets have cast a long shadow and many of their pronouncements, made thousands of years ago, still have acceptance today. And yet, their prophesies were taken largely from an inventory of ancient religious myths originally stocked by the most primitive societies. And the lives of many prophets betrayed symptoms of emotional problems characterized by the occurrence of delusions. It is remarkable in any event that these ancient prophets have found safe haven in our century.

The Persian prophet Zoroaster may have been the first of the great religious prophets, and he had an acknowledged effect on Jewish, Christian, and Muslim thought.

ZOROASTER

Zoroaster lived in ancient Persia. The original form of his name, Zarathustra, is believed to mean "possessor of camels." His date of birth is uncertain; scholars place him as early as 1400 or as late as 600 B.C.E.

Zoroaster was born into a religion that worshiped sun, moon, earth, fire, and water. Like a number of great religious leaders, Zoroaster was supposedly threatened by evil spirits when he was a child, but was saved. (Moses and Christ reportedly shared this experience.) Zoroaster became a priest of his religion and we are told had three wives and six children.

It was at the age of thirty that Zoroaster had the first in a series of visions. Perhaps significantly, they began at a critical time in his life when, as a priest, he was troubled by a number of religious questions. Some speculate that his visions were also helped by the inhalation of hemp fumes and the sacramental use of juice from the sacred haoma plant. In any event, his first vision took place by the banks of a river when an angel nine times the size of a man appeared before him and told Zoroaster that Ahura Mazda was the only true god and that he was to be his prophet. Further truths were revealed in subsequent visions. At first Zoroaster enjoyed very little success in preaching his message, but a turning point came when he received the support of the monarch named Vishtaspa. One of the legends is that Zoroaster converted Vishtaspa by curing the monarch's favorite horse of an indisposition. Zoroastrianism then became the religion of the mighty Persian Empire, which lasted for over one thousand years.

The influence of his teachings was felt in Judaism, Christianity, and Islam, all of which apparently accepted his notion of a Satan figure and angels. Of greater significance, Zoroaster taught the existence of a single god, whom he called Ahura Mazda. This differed from the teaching of Moses in the thirteenth century B.C.E., where Yahweh was proposed as the supreme god of the Hebrews but not as the only god and not as a universal god.

MOSES

Prophets such as Zoroaster or Muhammad appear in history books as real persons. Moses, however, although a figure in Bible stories, did not appear in any written history of the time (about 1300 B.C.E.). There is no mention of a Moses, for example, in any Egyptian source or other nonbiblical writing. This has led some scholars to believe that Moses was a mythical figure whose story was glorified as appropriate for the times and for the founder of the Hebrew state. In *Moses and Monotheism,* Sigmund Freud comments on this question:

> To deny a people the man whom it praises as the greatest of its sons is not a deed to be undertaken lightheartedly—especially by one belonging to that people. No consideration, however, will move me to set aside truth in favor of supposed national interests. Moreover, the elucidation of the mere facts of the problem may be expected to deepen our insight into the situation with which they are concerned.

The man Moses, the liberator of his people, who gave them their religion and their laws, belonged to an age so remote that the preliminary question arises whether he was a historical person or a legendary figure.[1]

The majority of historians would credit the existence of Moses, although not necessarily the popular accounts of his life story as reported in the Bible. The realities of his existence have been obscured by the centuries and by the religious myths that surround his person. In this case, Freud notes that "No historian can regard the Biblical account of Moses and the Exodus as other than a pious myth, which transformed a remote tradition in the interest of its own tendencies."[2]

Freud went on to suggest a very different perspective on Moses, including the surmise that Moses may have been an Egyptian of high rank, whose religious ideas came from the worshipers of an Egyptian sun-god, and whose leadership ended when he was murdered by his Hebrew followers. The god Yahweh was then proposed by a Midianite priest who was called Moses in order to preserve the legend. Freud suggested this in some detail, but as a hypothesis based on a logical construction of past events, not as a certainty. It serves to illustrate how little is known about Moses with historic certainty, and suggests that the biblical version should be approached with this in mind.

The fanciful nature of the Bible stories may be apparent, if not through the number of miracles, then through the mythic origins of stories that were reported as real. One example is the story of Moses put adrift in the bulrushes, now thought to have been taken from an earlier myth concerning Sargon, King of Agade, who founded Babylon about 2800 B.C.E. As it happened, this same myth, in its essence, attached itself not only to Moses but to more than a dozen other ancient personalities.

The Bible story, then, has the infant Moses adrift in an "ark of bulrushes" to escape the Egyptian king. The infant is found and saved by a princess, who then sees to his upbringing. On reaching manhood, Moses recognizes his heritage and is sympathetic to the plight of the Israelite slaves. In defense of one Israelite slave, Moses kills an Egyptian soldier simply by pronouncing the name of the Israelite god, Yahweh, and is then obliged to go into exile in the desert where he lives as a shepherd for forty years. Next, Yahweh again reveals himself to Moses in the form of a burning bush and Moses is given the task of leading the Israelites out of Egypt.

The Bible story continues with more miracles as the Israelite god, Yahweh, causes ten natural disasters to befall the land of Egypt—a hailstorm, a swarm of locusts, lice, a sandstorm, a pestilence, and more—until the Egyptian pharaoh is obliged to free the Israelites. These are described as miracles although today scholars suggest that such natural disasters were common to the area.

Other reported miracles included parting the waters of the Red Sea, drowning the Egyptian soldiers who followed, delivering the Ten Commandments, producing water from a rock and bread from heaven, glimpsing the Promised Land, and having God descend personally to claim Moses' soul.

In this century, of course, science does not credit miracles. And research has found that a number of pronouncements said to have come directly from God to Moses were instead taken from other cultures. For example, the originality of the Ten Commandments is questioned based on the discovery of Egyptian and Babylonian documents which show that similar rules existed at the time of, or before, the Israelite commandments. In the Egyptian Book of the Dead, for example, the dead man examines his conscience by asking:

I did not commit injustice;
I did not prey upon others;
I was not avaricious;
I did not steal;

I did not kill anyone;
I did not make the bushel smaller . . .
I did not rob from the possessions of the temple;
I did not speak a lie . . .
I did not dishonor (the) god. . . .

So many of the laws thought to have been given by God through Moses had already been established for centuries.

In the Bible story, Moses proposed Yahweh as the tribal god of the Hebrews. Yet it was the Hebrew prophets, centuries later, who finally persuaded the Hebrews to abandon other deities such as Baal, whose symbol was the bull, and to recognize Yahweh as the only god, and as a universal god.

HEBREW PROPHETS

The early Hebrew prophets were closely associated with the priesthood, but functioned primarily as oracles. They claimed to be in direct, personal contact with a deity and therefore could speak his words.

The concept was not unique to the time. Egyptian, Babylonian, and other priesthoods claimed similar prophetic powers. The prophet was said to come under the possession of a spirit and in that ecstatic state was able to talk with the god or gods of his religion. Some of the early Hebrew prophets talked with Yahweh (the god proposed by Moses) and others with Baal, the bull-god.

The state of ecstasy necessary for a prophetic statement was usually achieved by great physical exertion. The early Hebrew prophets used music, dancing, shouting, and intoxicating drinks as ways to induce prophetic ecstasy. In later times the prophets were given to a milder form of ecstasy, but the experience was still of a mystical character.

Prophet Ezekiel

The Hebrew prophet Ezekiel claimed the Spirit of the Lord often came upon him in trances. Etching by Ernst Fuchs.

Cincinnati Art Museum. Mr. and Mrs. Ron W. Sloniker Collection of 20th Century Biblical and Religious Prints.

The Hebrew prophets were not ordinary people, but mystics, and many of their actions would appear unusual today. Isaiah went naked and barefoot for three years. Jeremiah wore a wooden yoke of the type worn by oxen. Zedekiah wore a pair of iron horns. The prophet Saul was said to have stripped off his clothes, fallen on the floor, and lain naked for a day and a night. In this case there is no doubt that the temperament that leads to psychic experience has also led to insanity on occasion, as it did with Saul. Many strange actions were attributed to Ezekiel, whose prophecies were born in frenzied trances:

> Of the outstanding Israelite prophets, it was Ezekiel who experienced the phenomena of early prophetism in their most striking form. He was subject to frenzies in which he clapped his hands, stamped his feet, uttered inarticulate cries, and shook a sword to and fro. Trance experiences in which the spirit or hand of the Lord came upon him are frequent in his prophecies. On one occasion, as Ezekiel sat among a group of elders, he saw a figure of gleaming light and fire that put forth a hand, picked him up by a lock of hair and brought him to Jerusalem where he saw idolatries practiced in the temple.[3]

At the beginning, the Hebrew prophets asked a fee for their oracular services, and as professionals many banded together and lived in a commune. Some four hundred prophets of Yahweh could be consulted as a group, just as the Hebrew prophets serving Baal went about in bands of four hundred or more. Prophecy was to become even more commercial, but this was to change with prophets such as Elijah, Elisha, and Micah, who would speak their minds without apparent regard for personal gain or the opinions of their fellow prophets.

For many years the prophets of Yahweh contested the prophets of Baal, and in the end they prevailed. In the process their religious ideas evolved and became more universal in outlook, with greater emphasis on establishing a new social order. Some scholars hold that the later stages of Hebrew prophecy owe something to the Egyptian prophets of the time, both in literary style and in content. But to whatever extent the Egyptian prophets may have been influential, there is no doubt that the Hebrew prophets added a dimension to the religious thought of their time.

MUHAMMAD

No one has seriously questioned the existence of Muhammad as a historical figure. He was born in Mecca about 570. His father died before he was born and his mother died before he was six years of age. He was looked after by his grandfather and then an uncle, but grew up in dire poverty.

Muhammad was an illiterate. His youthful years were spent working as a camel driver and traveling throughout the Mideast, where he would have been exposed to the religions of the time— Zoroastrianism, Christianity, and Judaism.

During his years as a camel driver, Muhammad met and then married a wealthy widow who owned the caravan. He was twenty-five years old, she about forty years of age. Over a twenty-five-year marriage, they had two sons and four daughters.

After this marriage, Muhammad was rich and respected, but he became troubled emotionally and spent more time in the desert away from his business and family. During these periods of meditation in the desert, the angel Gabriel was said to have appeared and brought him a message from God. Although Muhammad was illiterate, the angel commanded him to read and he did so. Muhammad became convinced that he was a prophet of God, following Abraham, Moses, Jesus, and others—but enjoying the final revelation.

When Muhammad first began preaching in Mecca, his ideas were not widely welcomed. So in an attempt to win over the Jewish population, Muhammad commanded the Muslims to face Jerusalem when praying. However, antagonisms between them increased and Muslims were then ordered to pray toward Mecca.

After his wife died, Muhammad moved to Medina and married the nine-year-old daughter of a friend. In Medina, Muhammad gained a following and became powerful both as a religious and political head. He then began armed raids against Mecca and eventually was able to conquer the city with a force of ten thousand warriors. With his victory, Muhammad rode his camel to the center of the pilgrimage in Mecca, raised himself in the saddle, and proclaimed a new era where Allah would rule supreme. Although the conqueror, he respected the Black Stone of Mecca, which Islamic legend says fell from heaven during the time of Adam and Eve, and with this show of reverence was able to unify the Arabian people in his Islamic religion.

Muhammad married a number of new wives, some of whom helped to strengthen his political relationships. Among the marriages, he was criticized for marrying the wife of his adopted son, an act that was considered incestuous by the Arab culture of the time. Muhammad died at the age of sixty-two.

Muhammad, like other prophets, has been challenged concerning the authenticity of his divine inspiration. Some historians have suggested that his inspiration was due to epilepsy or hallucinations.

In most religions, then, it has been the religious prophets—the men who claim to talk with gods—who have been responsible for the selection or discovery of a particular god and for providing a description of his divine nature and powers.

Prophecy has also served to establish rules of social behavior that appear divine in their origin and are therefore unassailable. Freud noted the role of prophecy in ancient Israel:

the people of Israel had believed themselves to be the favorite children of God, and when the great Father caused misfortune after misfortune to rain down upon this people of his, they were never shaken in their belief of his relationship to them or questioned his power or righteousness. Instead, they produced the prophets, who held up their sinfulness before them; and out of their sense of guilt they created the over-strict commandments of their priestly religion.[4]

The credibility of the ancient religious prophets is open to question on many counts, one of which is their behavior. Modern psychologists have studied their actions, in a rearview mirror, and in some cases found symptoms of schizophrenia and epilepsy, and the possibility of delusions through sensory deprivation. But accurate analyses are difficult given the separation in time and the differences in culture.

The trances themselves were techniques and not necessarily indicative of mental disorder:

Possession and trance in religious ceremonies are ways of approaching the supernatural by reproducing psychopathological states. The techniques for inducing possession and ecstatic trance are intended to produce artificially hallucinations, hysterical crises and similar phenomena. However, the participants in these rites are not all abnormal; some are true neurotics, or afflicted with some other mental disorder, others are normal individuals.[5]

On this basis, it would appear that the faithful must make their own determination of the mental state of their prophets on an individual basis.

To the advantage of the ancient prophets, it must be remembered that most people of that time shared a belief in prophecy and unseen spirits. The prophet simply went the next step and offered to act as an agent, or conduit, for communications with these spirits. In this sense, their behavior may not be judged aberrant.

An example is given that in Haiti many people believe in the power of voodoo priests to enter into trances, and thus occupied to converse with the spirit world. The belief may appear strange, and the antics of the priest bizarre, but neither the Haitian priest nor the public would thereby be judged insane. Similarly, Christians and Jews have long believed in the power of their prophets to converse with spirits via ecstatic trances, and may regard the frenzied actions of their prophets as the accepted religious behavior of the time, not as abnormal.

Finally, the credibility of religious prophecy does not rest on the mental state of the prophet, be it aberrant or not, but on the reasonableness of the concept itself. Prophecy first requires a belief in spirits which today's science does not support. And then, confidence in an ancient prophet who, while in a trance, has a vision seen by him alone. That this is a questionable foundation for enduring religious belief is most apparent, perhaps, in the collection of bull-gods, buffalo-gods, and the thousands of other conjurations which prophecy has produced.

Prophets, then, like gods are creatures of a culture. And people who wish to believe in unknown spirits are then required to believe that certain men and women have been chosen to act as their spokespersons, otherwise their gods are mute. The concept of prophecy is certainly less viable today, and the evangelist who hears voices or has visions might be viewed with some concern by a more worldly audience. Religious tradition nevertheless sustains a belief in the ancient prophets who heard the voice or had a vision of their ancient god. And today our most fundamental religious beliefs have come from those voices, those visions, those prophets.

NOTES

1. Sigmund Freud, *Moses and Monotheism* (New York: Vintage Books, 1967), p. 3.

2. Ibid., p. 38.

3. George Rosen, *Madness in Society* (New York: Harper and Row, 1969), p. 53.

4. Sigmund Freud, *Civilization and Its Discontents* (New York: W. W. Norton and Company, 1961), p. 74.

5. Rosen, *Madness in Society,* p. 57.

7

Priests:
All about Vocations

I n earlier societies the local priest was a figure of great importance in the community. Food, water, and all of the essentials for survival were under the control of the gods, and the gods were under the control of the priest. If they were not, then the priest would be driven off or killed and a new one found.

At first the gods were controlled by magic. Humans believed that spells and charms could compel the gods to act in a certain way, but over the centuries it became apparent that the gods would not be intimidated, so humans changed their approach to entreaty, or religion. When magic turned into religion, the magicians turned into priests.

EARLY SOCIETIES

Early priests were often chosen on the basis of a distinctive physical appearance or temperament. Outward signs such as a deformity or a particularly unattractive appearance led some societies to nominate the unfortunate for a priestly vocation. Siberian tribes, for example, interpreted fainting or dizzy spells as evidence of a vocation, and tribes from many continents viewed shivering and shaking in like manner. *The Encyclopaedia of Religion and Ethics* describes the importance of an unusual temperament: "The mental disposition which is supposed to qualify a person for the priestly office reveals a very important feature of early priesthood. Among a great number of peoples the priests must display a considerable excitability of temperament; consequently certain qualifications of a pathological and psychological nature generally characterize the priests and sorcerers of uncivilized races. From several parts of the world we are informed that individuals of an eccentric disposition are considered to be specially apt for the sacerdotal vocation."[1]

In the case of both prophets and priests, early humans attached a great deal of importance to any actions which seemed to suggest a divine visitation. By definition, actions that were beyond their capacity to understand were the work of spirits. So those who were subject to convulsive fits were often thought to be possessed by the gods. So also were people who went into self-induced ecstatic trances such as those associated with the early Hebrew prophets and the Greek oracles, among others.

> It is natural to the savage mind to ascribe ecstasy to spiritual agency. The convulsive gestures and incoherent utterances of the inspired seem to show that his own will is absent, and that some strange being has taken possession of his body. A spirit or god is therefore supposed to speak through his mouth and to command his actions. This faculty of falling into an ecstatic condition is all the more necessary for would-be priests, as among savage peoples manifestations of a prophetic or divine delirium do almost universally accompany religious ceremonies.
>
> The observation that an ecstatic disposition is universally

associated with priesthood draws attention to the fact that in many cases insane persons are looked upon with superstitious awe. The main distinction between insanity and ecstasy seems to be that the former is generally ascribed to a permanent, the latter to a more casual, possession by a spirit. Some people believe the insane to be under the influence of demons, while others assume that they are inspired by good spirits. In conformity with the latter idea, great veneration is paid to the insane, who are also sometimes thought to possess the spirit of prophecy.[2]

Ecstatic trances and visions were sometimes the result of emotional problems, but could also be induced by fasting or frenzied behavior. Natives of some American, African, and Asian tribes encouraged visions by partaking of substances such as flybane, strong tobacco juice, and plants which are now known to produce hallucinatory effects.

There were other criteria for the selection of priests. Some societies believed that priests were selected by the gods, who let their intentions be known to humans. The Moxo in Brazil, for example, required that their priests be attacked and wounded by a jaguar, the animal they worshiped as a god. Some Asian cultures believed that being struck by lightning was a clear sign of divine favor—in which case the son of the departed would be elected to the priesthood. At other times the priest was able to gain the confidence of his tribe simply by his superior cunning in predicting the future.

The priests held power by their knowledge, showmanship, and the cultivated superstitions of the lay religious. In many cases, the priest was the most knowledgeable person in the community. He had studied the healing properties of plants, he understood some of the recurring cycles of nature, and he was acquainted with the habits of certain animals. This intelligence was used to establish his authority over the people. In some cases his superior intelligence enabled him to engage in prophecy, on occasion in collusion with other interested parties. Prophecies that did not work out despite his precautions were explained as whims of the gods or the actions of evil spirits. Since the priest worked directly with the gods and in an atmosphere of great mystery, his explanation for nonperformance was usually accepted.

Fear was also a hold over the people. Priests described the gods as ill-disposed toward humans, and the dangers inherent in life at that time must have supported that point of view. As the one best equipped to deal with such dangerous gods, the priest was as feared as he was respected. The priest often dressed in a bizarre and frightening costume, painted his body in strange designs, and let it be known that nonbelievers would be punished by the spirits that he controlled. His involvement in ecstatic orgies and the fury of his preparation for these events also inspired fear among his tribe.

It was customary for priests to distinguish themselves from ordinary people. Throughout most cultures, priests adopted distinctive costumes and either let their hair grow or shaved the head. Fasting and similar observances have marked the priestly life and in some cases, celibacy. There were other cases where priests have been disposed to take sexual liberties of an extraordinary nature. *The Encyclopaedia of Religion and Ethics* also notes: "A remarkable fact is that the priests almost universally distinguish themselves from the community at large by means of a separate language which they use in the divine service or in intercourse with each other" (p. 283).

There were undoubtedly impostors and opportunists among the early priests. From today's vantage point it seems apparent that many of the priestly actions were calculated to strengthen their own positions of importance and privilege at the expense of others. But it is also apparent that many priests may have acted in the sincere belief that they could influence, if not control, the gods and secure advantages for themselves and their tribes.

CIVILIZED SOCIETIES

Babylonian

A Babylonian priesthood was in existence over four thousand years ago. Membership in the priesthood brought with it great wealth and influence. Many of the priests were trained in temple schools where they developed specializations in sacrifices, healing, interpreting dreams, or divining the future. Among other powers, the priests of Babylon were empowered to forgive sins, which made them very valuable to a society frequently in trouble with the wind-god and the sun-god. Priestly functions that are conducted today were conducted by the tonsured, robed priests of Babylon: anointing heads, purifying sites, saying prayers, writing sacred books, forgiving sins, and reporting miracles. The high priests were in close communication with the king who himself served as the great high priest of the religion.

Egyptian

Also thousands of years before Christ, the Egyptian civilization was very advanced and its priesthood reflected the complex social structure. The Egyptian king was the high priest over all other priests, but he was also a god—not merely a representative but a manifestation of the great god Horus. The king was later thought to be the physical embodiment of the sun-god, as well, and thus was in an ideal position to act as a mediator between the people of Egypt and their many divinities. Priests of lower rank performed many functions, serving as judges, musicians, physicians, and in mortuaries and temples. The temple was the house of a particular god and the priesthood was in some respects the domestic help; in services performed daily, the priest sprinkled water on an idol of the god, fumigated the god with incense, clothed him, anointed him, and applied cosmetics to his features. It reflected a belief that gods lived as humans did and required the same bodily preparations to meet the new day.

Hebrew

The Hebrew religious sanctuaries of three thousand years ago contained both priests and prophets. The priests were responsible for guarding the gold and silver valuables in the sanctuary and for interpreting the words of the oracle. A teaching function was also a primary responsibility of the priest and in pursuing this role the priest became accepted as a judge. Sacrificial duties were not, apparently, a part of the very early Hebrew priesthood, as most adult males were themselves capable of performing sacrificial ceremonies. In time, however, sacrificial duties became the primary function of the priest.

The Temple of Jerusalem was served by many priests—so many that a rotation was initiated to give each priest the opportunity to fulfill his priestly function. To qualify for the Hebrew priesthood, applicants had to be free of bodily defects; a listing of one hundred and forty blemishes served as checkpoints for physical examinations. Priests were not allowed to own land and their remuneration was derived from offerings and redemptions. A firstborn son had to be redeemed by payment, which went to the officiating priest. Priests were also entitled to the skins of the larger sacrificial animals and the breast and right shoulder of smaller animals. Many Jewish priests were quite poor as a result of this system of remuneration, but it was nevertheless their duty to assure the high priest of a handsome income in keeping with his position. Finally, the destruction of the Temple of Jerusalem by the Romans posed too great a hardship on the Jewish priesthood and most of the functions of the priest were replaced by family tradition.

Zoroastrian

Zoroastrian priests became known as the Magi, from the name of an ancient tribe or caste. The priests performed sacrifices, when not forbidden, and officiated at all public worship. A primary responsibility was tending the sacred fire and preparing the sacred haoma plant for consumption by the priests. The juice of the haoma plant is generally thought to have possessed hallucinogenic properties. Fees were charged for certain ceremonies but as they were not adequate compensation the priests were allowed to take on outside work, very often healing. Their symbols of office were a cloth to cover the face, a leather strap to kill unclean insects, a knife to kill snakes, and a bundle of twigs from the sacred cedar tree.

Greek

Ancient Greece did not have a formal priesthood wherein only a certain class of men could mediate with the gods. The Hellenic attitude supposed that men should be involved in various pursuits and not restricted in their endeavors. Aristotle suggested, for example, that a man might become a soldier, statesman, and priest in that order. There was nevertheless a recognition that certain people were especially gifted in some religious areas. Since women were thought to have special powers as mediums, the oracles at Delphi were priestesses. Where priests or priestesses were required to take care of temples they served a single god at a particular shrine, rather than exercising a broader religious role. The result was that lay people were largely responsible for their own destinies in terms of pleasing the many gods.

Roman

The qualifications for Roman priesthood were Roman citizenship, a clean civil record, free birth, and an absence of physical infirmities. The powers of the priests were under the control of the Senate, although the priesthood was independent except in unusual circumstances; many of the priests also had civic and military offices. Unlike the Greek priesthood, the organization of the Roman priesthood was intricate and seemingly interminable, ranging from the Vestal virgins who looked after the sacred fire to Magistrate priests who looked after the sacred chickens. Briefly considered, the six Vestal Virgins performed many ceremonies throughout the year but were primarily responsible for keeping the sacred fire lit; they began at age six or eight, served for thirty years and remained chaste during their tenure under penalty of being buried alive. The sacred chickens were one of five ways to predict whether a given action would be favorably regarded by the gods. This kind of priestly divination was called *disciplina auguralis* and, among other uses, was considered by the military before launching an attack: "The chickens were brought in cages, and, after the general who was to take the auspices had placed himself at the door of the tent within the bounds of the templum, they were let out. He observed their manner of walking and especially the way in which they ate the food that was thrown to them. The most favourable omen that they could give (*auspicium solistinum*) was to let pieces of food fall from their beaks. When such an omen was wanted, it was easily obtained either by giving the chickens crumbly food or by starving them before they were liberated and so causing a degree of haste in eating that resulted in numerous manifestations of the kind desired."[3]

Other auguries involved interpreting the flight and cries of wild birds and the presence of thunder and lightning. At that time, then, Christianity was introduced to a credulous population.

Christian

The early Christian ministry included both itinerant and local activities. Apostles, prophets, and evangelists came under the itinerant category; bishops, presbyters, and deacons performed local administrative and pastoral duties. The bishop of Rome in 251 C.E. listed the following orders and classes:[4]

one	bishop
46	presbyters
7	deacons
7	subdeacons
42	acolytes
52	exorcists, readers, doorkeepers
1500	widows and distressed persons

The Christian religion maintained that its priesthood did not deny the lay person access to the deity and taught that any individual could commune with God. The early priesthood, nevertheless, was routinely called on to heal injuries and illnesses through the laying on of hands, to remove evil spirits through exorcistic formulas, to foretell events through its powers of prophecy, and to interpret the wishes of the Almighty with respect to social and religious mores. From this standpoint, the priesthood was a desirable, if not necessary, adjunct to the Christian God, and the priesthood exercised great influence over the lives of individuals and the institutions of society.

In later years Catholics and Protestants were to disagree on the function of the priesthood. Roman Catholics believe the priest's principal function is the sacrament of the Eucharist (i.e., the sharing of bread and wine which are sacramentally associated with the body and blood of Christ), with secondary emphasis on teaching. For Protestants teaching is the fundamental responsibility; the word "priest" was supplanted by the title "minister" or "pastor" in most Protestant denominations.

Islamic

There was never an established priesthood in the Islamic religion. On Friday of each week the Muslim is required to visit a mosque and pray. The prayers are led by an imam, who is not a priest but simply a pious member of the community. On other days a muezzin climbs to the top of the minaret and calls out for the faithful to pray wherever they may be. This prayer is repeated five times during each day.

Indian

In India, the priesthood belonged to a special class from the earliest of times and was hereditary in character. The Brahmins were in the service of kings and noblemen and were well paid for their religious efforts. They did not at first claim to be gods; this description of themselves was to come later. Certainly they enjoyed the highest respect—not even the king could censure a Brahmin, and the fine for striking a Brahmin was one thousand cows. The Brahmins claimed special abilities to win the favor of the gods, and used both human sacrifice and songs to achieve their ends. The soma-sacrifice was an important part of their ritual; the juice of the Indian soma plant may have been fermented and possibly had hallucinogenic properties to aid in the communication godwards. The Brahmins believed that a sacrifice compelled the gods to comply and they were prepared, if need be, to punish the gods or even create new ones. Among the more potent sacrifices was one in which the worshiper bestowed all his earthly possessions on the priest.

Brahmin priests oversee the temples and the idols of the gods, which are awakened, washed, dressed, and fed to the music of temple bells and the smell of incense and flowers. Other Brahmin priests are members of religious schools and are accorded great respect, even to the point of being viewed as the embodiments of the gods. By virtue of their mantras, or spells, and magical powers, some Brahmin are even regarded as superior to the gods. According to a four-stage plan in life, Brahmin priests begin their priesthood with study, followed by years of sacrifice and charities, then asceticism, and end their days in meditation.

Jainist

Brahminism in India fostered two new schools of thought which became separate religions, Jainism and Buddhism. From the first, Jainist monks placed great weight on ascetic approaches and paid great reverence to all life, even the life of insects. Vows to renounce all personal property led the Mahavira sect to abandon all clothes. The duty of the Jainist monk was to become a homeless wanderer and spend his time in meditation and spiritual exercises, although some sects also practice temple worship and wash, feed, and clothe the gods of the temple. Jainist monks are still encouraged to depart this world through a religious suicide.

Buddhist

The Buddhist religion spread throughout China and Japan and the Far East. Whatever the country, Buddhist priests serve mostly as educators and advisors on matters of religion. They have never acted as mediators between people and gods nor officiated at sacrificial rites, which have been condemned by the Buddhist religion. Followers are encouraged to find salvation through their own efforts or, if a Mahayanist Buddhist, with the help of saints or semidivine beings who renounced Nirvana to help others attain salvation. In either case, the priest has no direct role and the worshiper is personally responsible for his deliverance. As an aid to the worshiper, however, Buddhist monks introduced a formal confession of sins into their religious duties.

Chinese

Even before Confucianism, Taoism, and Buddhism, ancient China was given to shamanism and ancestor worship. The primitive shamans were called wu and functioned to invoke the spirits of the dead, engage in prophecy, and exorcise evil spirits. The wu were possessed by spirits of Yang, whose light and warmth neutralized the darkness of the Yin elements. They were retained by worshipers to cast spells and paid to perform "life-plucking," which meant dismembering a living body so that its parts could be used in sorcery. About 500 B.C.E., China first embraced Confucianism, which is regarded more as a moral or ethical system than a religion, and Taoism. The Taoist priests may be married or single, and may live in their own dwelling and wear the native dress of the country. Many Taoist priests are itinerant and support themselves by selling charms. Their field of specialization is astrology and alchemy, which has widespread appeal among the peasant class. At least claiming to be a part of the Taoist priesthood are the saikong, who are involved in sacrificial practices and exorcism.

To summarize, in many indigenous cultures it was believed that magic spells and charms could compel the spirits to act in an advantageous manner. When the approach did not prove serviceable, presumably, intimidation changed to entreaty, or religion. And when magic turned into religion, the magicians turned into priests.

The ancient priests were presumed to have special powers which enabled them to influence the actions of the spirits. Such powers were often thought to be apparent in aberrant behavior, which was taken as a strong indication that a person was possessed by spirits and therefore a logical candidate to deal with the spirit world.

Clearly, many of the priests in indigenous societies preyed upon the superstitions of the people to gain advantages for themselves and their religions. But it also seems apparent that many functioned in the sincere belief that they could influence a spirit world and call down blessings on themselves and their community.

In ancient civilizations the priests became representatives of their respective gods. Some gave themselves supernatural power, such as the priest-kings of Egypt, and others were content with their status as humans. But all enjoyed insights into the nature of their gods, and proficiency in the rituals of their religion, which brought them social position and the power that was implicit in fellowship with a god.

Overall, there has been very little change in the role of priests. Ancient priests and prophets gave us many of our current religious beliefs, which were preserved by sacred book, ritual, and the tradition of the priesthood. Indeed, as noted, many of the priestly functions of today were conducted by the tonsured, robed priests of Babylon some four thousand years ago: anointing heads, purifying sites, saying prayers, making sacrifices, writing sacred books, forgiving sins, and reporting miraculous occurrences.

NOTES

1. James Hastings, ed., "Priests," *The Encyclopaedia of Religion and Ethics* (New York: Charles Scribner and Sons, 1951), p. 281.

2. Ibid.

3. Ibid., p. 331.

4. Ibid., "Ministry," p. 665.

8

Holy Books:
As Textbooks on Science

oly books are a fundamental part of every religion. Along with the traditions of the priesthood, it is the holy book that provides a lasting description of the god and his intentions, as well as his instructions to the faithful. Some religions view their holy book as the literal words of a god, while others believe their book is inspired by a god, although written by men and women. Whichever the interpretation, historically the contents of the books are unassailable in the eyes of the faithful and not subject to doctrinal error or historical inaccuracy.

Of course, as religion itself was born of societies over ten thousand years ago, so were many holy books written in ancient cultural settings, given to the fanciful stories of their time, and inhibited by a lack of knowledge available to more modern cultures. So the holy books were the thoughts of people who believed in mythical heroes, marauding spirits, and magic in its many forms. Sticks could be turned into snakes, demons concealed in human bodies, people returned from the dead, and lightning called down from on high. And Paradise beckoned, with winged angels to welcome the virtuous to a condition of eternal bliss—or so it was believed by the faithful.

For almost two thousand years, Christians in all walks of life took the Bible to be literally true. Whatever their educational background or personal experience, people believed that the Bible was the literal word of God and therefore not subject to question or challenge. Did Jonah live in the body of a great fish? Was Eve created from Adam's rib? Would the world's animals fit into a home-made ark? Was there really a magic garden and a talkative snake? The answer was yes if it said so in the Bible—or if theologians so interpreted the words of the Bible.

The literal interpretation of the Bible necessarily gave rise to many mistaken views of the universe. And of course a young science was often frustrated by the Church's insistence that any new findings support the teachings of the Bible. In fact, there was little science of any kind because the Church undertook to answer all questions concerning the nature of the universe by recourse to its holy book. Thus a "sacred science" was created and the Bible was viewed as the only valid source of knowledge. Saint Augustine (354–430) gave words to this belief in his declaration:

> Nothing is to be accepted save on the authority of Scripture, since greater is that authority than all the powers of the human mind.

Saint Augustine's message was a clear statement of the Church's belief that all truth and knowledge flowed from the Bible, which had been vested with these qualities by a holy ghost. And for more than a thousand years thereafter the Church resisted any ideas that did not conform to Scripture and enhance the authority of the Church. Thus scientists like Copernicus, Galileo, and others were frustrated in their attempts to explain natural phenomena by natural causes.

Today scholars recognize many inconsistencies in the Bible beginning with the early history of humans as recounted in Genesis. For example, one account of Genesis spoke of the six days of Creation, each with a morning and an evening, and a daily record of accomplishment. The second account of Genesis spoke of a single day only with Creation as an instantaneous act.

In his book *Folklore in the Old Testament,* Sir James Frazer notes a "striking discrepancy" between the two accounts of the creation of man in the first and second chapters of Genesis: "In the first narrative the deity begins with fishes and works steadily up through birds and beasts to man and woman. In the second narrative he begins with man and works downward through the lower animals to woman, who apparently marks the nadir of divine workmanship."[1] So Frazer notes the order of merit is reversed and in the second version woman is fashioned as a mere afterthought from a rib taken while Adam was asleep. The discrepancy between the two versions may be ascribed to indifferent editing which failed to note the obvious contradiction of the two accounts. Noteworthy also in the Jehovistic Document is the author's attitude toward woman, who, Frazer suggests, "hardly attempts to hide his deep contempt for woman. The lateness of her creation and the irregular and undignified manner of it—made out of a piece of her lord and master, after all the lower animals had been created in a regular and decent manner—sufficiently mark the low opinion he held of her nature; and in the sequel his misogynism, as we may fairly call it, takes a still darker tinge, when he ascribes all the misfortunes and sorrows of the human race to the credulous folly and unbridled appetite of its first mother."[2]

We may take it, then, that the Bible opens with two conflicting accounts of creation, a concern which is only heightened by the failure of the editor to acknowledge the discrepancy. In the second account, moreover, the author appears to be a misogynist whose views were given standing by their inclusion in the Bible, with a consequence that women have been a casualty of his thinking ever since.

Beyond the errors and inconsistencies which have been found in the Bible, scholarship has revealed that many of its stories come from folklore. An example cited by Frazer is the biblical conception that man was modeled out of clay, as a figure might be modeled by a potter. This conception of man's creation was shared by a number of earlier religions, as Frazer notes: "From various allusions in Babylonian literature it would seem that the Babylonians also conceived man to have been moulded out of clay. . . . In Egyptian mythology Khnoumou, the father of the gods, is said to have moulded man out of clay on his potter's wheel. . . . So in Greek legend the sage Prometheus is said to have moulded the first men out of clay at Panopeus in Phocis."[3] And Frazer goes on to conclude that "such rude conceptions of the origin of mankind, common to Greeks, Hebrews, Babylonians, and Egyptians, were handed down to the civilized peoples of antiquity by their early or barbarous forefathers. In fact, tribes from the Pacific islands, Asia, Africa, and even America shared the belief that the first man must have been moulded from clay."[4] So the Bible does not offer an original concept of man's creation, but merely relies on the folklore that was extant. The idea of a creation out of clay no doubt arose because in earlier days people were unable to visualize their gods in terms other than their own recognized abilities—and so their gods must have modeled shapes from clay as they themselves were wont to do. And yet Christianity accepted the story as literal truth, and for the better part of two thousand years.

One of the best-known stories in the Bible, that of Adam and Eve, also came to the Old Testament by way of ancient folklore. The same symbolism of a magic garden and talking serpent were seen in the earliest cuneiform texts, shown on Sumerian cylinder seals, and recounted in the folklore of earlier people long before the biblical account of Adam and Eve. The purpose of the "Fall" legend throughout the world was simply to explain the existence of evil and human suffering in a world supposedly under the protection of a beneficent god. The "Fall" made humanity accountable for the problems in the world and thereby preserved the image of a capable and caring Creator. The consequences were far-reaching for Adam, Eve, and others, as Frazer summarized:

> learning from the abashed couple how they had disobeyed his command by eating of the fruit of the tree of knowledge, he flew into a towering passion. He cursed the serpent, condemning him to go on his belly, to eat dust, and to be the enemy of mankind all the days of his life: he cursed the ground, condemning it to bring forth thorns and thistles; he cursed the woman, condemning her to bear children in sorrow and to be in subjection to her husband: he cursed the man, condemning him to wring his daily bread from the ground in the sweat of his brow, and finally to return to the dust out of which he had been taken. Having relieved his feelings by these copious maledictions, the irascible but really kindhearted deity relented so far as to make coats of skins for the culprits to replace their scanty apron of fig-leaves; and clad in these new garments the shamefaced pair retreated among the trees, while in the west the sunset died away and the shadows deepened on Paradise Lost.[5]

Remarkably, the story of Adam and Eve was credited as literal truth until the middle of the twentieth century. It is now viewed by scholars as an ancient myth, perhaps instructional on the level of a nursery tale.

In its symbolism, the particular story of the serpent and the magic garden has been found in folklore around the world, although there were also other settings which served to explain the problems of life. The prophet Zoroaster preached a Fall in the ancient Persian religion, wherein the god Ahura Mazda created a perfect world entirely free of pain and despair, only to have his perfect creation marred by an opposing evil spirit, Augra Minju, who brought about a Fall and introduced evil and ignorance into the world. Greek mythology also had its legend of a Fall wherein Hesiod (8th century B.C.E.) reported that men in the most ancient times were "a golden race" who lived like gods without care—but then came Pandora, the first woman, who opened a box bidden by divine command to remain closed, and let loose a torrent of troubles into the world.

Clearly, many cultures have had difficulty in reconciling the ills of the world with the goodness of their gods, and were left with no real alternative than to absolve the gods and shoulder the blame.

Another curiosity in the Old Testament concerns the mark of Cain. In Genesis, after Cain murdered his brother Abel he became an outcast, but his remonstrations with God were rewarded with a distinctive mark that protected him from assailants. This may have derived from the mark many tribal members wore as a protection, as it signified that their death would surely be avenged by their tribe. Frazer speculated that, in this case, the mark may have been a protection against his brother's ghost.

> This explanation of the mark of Cain has the advantage of relieving the Biblical narrative from a manifest absurdity. For on the usual interpretation God affixed the mark to Cain in order to save him from human assailants, apparently forgetting that there was nobody to assail him, since the earth was as yet inhabited only by the murderer himself and his parents. Hence, by

assuming that the foe of whom the first murderer went in fear
was a ghost instead of a living man, we avoid the irreverence of
imparting the deity a grave lapse of memory little in keeping
with divine omniscience.[6]

The legend of the great flood in the Book of Genesis once again
reveals two different versions of the account, marked by inconsistencies, which were later combined to form a single story. One version noted a distinction between clean and unclean animals of
those invited aboard, while the other writer made no such distinction. One version suggested that the flood lasted sixty-one days,
the other noted a duration of twelve months and ten days. In one
account the flood was caused by rain, in the other both rain and
water from subterranean sources was responsible. An altar and
sacrifice were mentioned in one version but not the other.

Moreover, it was found that the Hebrew story was apparently
taken from a Babylonian flood story which preceded the Hebrew
account by eleven or twelve centuries. Frazer noted:

A very cursory comparison of the Hebrew with the Babylonian
account of the Deluge may suffice to convince us that the two
narratives are not independent, but that one of them must be
derived from the other, or both from a common original. The
points of resemblance between the two are far too numerous and
detailed to be accidental. In both narratives the divine powers
resolve to destroy mankind by a great flood; in both the secret is
revealed beforehand to a man by a god, who directs him to build
a great vessel, in which to save himself and seed of every kind.
It is probably no mere accidental coincidence that in the Babylonian story, as reported by Berosus, the hero saved from the
flood was the *tenth* King of Babylon, and that in the Hebrew
story Noah, was the *tenth* man in descent from Adam. In both
narratives the favoured man, thus warned of God, builds a huge

vessel in several stories, makes it water-tight with pitch or bitumen, and takes into it his family and animals of all sorts: in both, the deluge is brought about in large measure by heavy rain, and lasts for a greater or less number of days: in both, all mankind are drowned except the hero and his family: in both, the man sends forth birds, a raven and a dove, to see whether the water of the flood has abated: in both, the dove after a time returns to the ship because it could find no place in which to rest: in both, the raven does not return: in both, the vessel at last grounds on a mountain: in both, the hero, in gratitude for his rescue, offers sacrifice on the mountain: in both, the gods smell the sweet savour, and their anger is appeased.[7]

Following the account reported in Genesis, other adornments to the story were conceived by the Hebrews. It was said that, prior to the flood, people led a life of consummate ease, wherein one sowing would produce a harvest that would last forty years; wherein magic arts could compel the sun and moon to do the Hebrews' bidding; and where children were in their mother's womb only a few days and after birth they could immediately walk, talk, and fend off demons. It was also said that God warned the Hebrews of an impending punishment by having the sun rise in the west and set in the east for a seven-day period. These and other embellishments to the flood story illustrate the proclivity to enhance the narrative for popular consumption, as indeed many Bible stories were punctuated with miraculous happenings.

Finally, Frazer reports that similar stories of floods were rampant in the ancient world and among earlier peoples, all thought to be the work of the gods and many sharing the same elements as the Hebrew story and the earlier Babylonian legend from which it was taken. The Babylonian legend itself appears to have been derived from a still more ancient Sumerian legend. So the story in Genesis was far from original in the telling.

Medieval Scribe

A scribe in his monastery workshop, shown copying a sacred text, before the fifteenth-century invention of the printing press.

Medieval French manuscript. Bibliotheque National de France, Paris.

The concluding episode in Genesis, which relates to the general history of humankind, is the legend of the Tower of Babel. The Bible has it that God became jealous when he saw that humans were building a tower so high that it threatened to encroach on his own preserve, and so he confounded the builders by giving them different languages and proceeded to scatter them about the earth. As it happened, however, the Hebrew explanation for the origin of language appears to have come from the Chaldeans, who predated the Hebrews. The Chaldeans apparently built a tower for astronomical observations, but through faulty construction it toppled over—the Chaldeans chose to believe it was the work of a jealous god. The Chaldeans and then the Hebrews chose a tower for their language myth because in ancient times it was assumed that the gods lived above the clouds and people wished to build their altars as near to the gods as possible. The same thinking prompted the Hindus to choose a high tree and the Mexicans the great Pyramid of Cholula for their language myths, both of which explained the differences in language around the world as the work of jealous gods. The Tower myth, then, is another belief that came to Jews and Christians not as an original concept, but as one borrowed from earlier religions and primitive peoples. Still, by virtue of being in the Bible the Tower story was accepted for several thousand years and only recently became recognized as myth.

So, although the Bible was once held to be infallible and the only valid source of knowledge, it is now apparent that the Old Testament was a very human undertaking with a generous measure of editing errors and other inconsistencies in the material. And many of the stories which formed the basis for our religious beliefs, and explained the human condition overall, were not original but were myths adopted from ancient civilizations or early peoples. The stories of Creation, Adam and Eve, the Great Deluge, and the Tower of Babel are representative of the many Bible stories that were dipped from the vast reservoir of ancient religious myth.

And yet acknowledging the possibility of error took almost two thousand years—seemingly a long time to conclude that many Bible stories were fanciful creations. The explanation is in the authority of the Church, the weight of tradition, and perhaps the comfort afforded by the familiar. The power of our social coercive is apparent in such prolonged beliefs, and the social construction of reality.

Still, one may wonder why people in all walks of life would believe in a literal garden of Eden, a serpent that could talk, and a fruit with marvelous properties. And for thousands of years. But such is the nature of myths and legends and, as Joseph Campbell says: "Today we know—know right well—that there was never anything of the kind: no garden of Eden anywhere on this earth, no time when the serpent could talk, no prehistoric 'Fall,' no exclusion from the garden, no universal flood, no Noah's Ark. The entire history on which our leading occidental religions have been founded is an anthology of fictions. But these are fictions of a type that have had—curiously enough—a universal vogue as the founding legends of other religions, too. Their counterparts have turned up everywhere—and yet, there was never such a garden, serpent, tree or deluge."[8]

The authorship and origin of New Testament narratives have also been the subject of considerable research in recent years. The latest conclusions, in a 1990 article "Who Wrote the Bible?" suggest that the issue is still in doubt. The following excerpts indicate the scope of the question and the uncertainties that surround the New Testament:[9]

Who Wrote the Bible?

It is the foundation of the Christian faith. On its words rest the very existence of the church and the hope of salvation for believers through the ages. Many consider it the only dependable and abiding revelation of God to humanity. Yet the New Testament, in many ways, is a mysterious and enigmatic collection of writings—one that has entranced, enthralled and perplexed scholars and theologians for nearly 2,000 years.

It is often called "The New Testament of Our Lord and Savior Jesus Christ." But Jesus didn't write a word of it. And while some of the writings bear the names of those who walked with Him on the dusty roads of Judea, centuries of scholarship have turned up little convincing evidence that His 12 closest disciples did much writing either.

The Christian Canon

It would be nearly a century after the death of Jesus before the concept of "Christian Scripture"—something as revered as the Old Testament had been for the Jews—would begin to emerge in the fledgling church. And it would take longer still before any consensus would arise as to which writings should be included in the canon—the sacred books officially sanctioned by church leaders.

. . . In part, the delay reflected the relatively slow development of Christian literature. As the Gospels tell it, Jesus assured His followers before He ascended to heaven that one day He would return for them. His disciples took that to mean within a few years. So when they set out to preach His message in Jerusalem and Judea, with His words and deeds still vivid memories, they gave little thought to writing for posterity. They simply taught as they remembered. And those whom they taught, in turn taught others.

The Four Gospels

They are regarded by many as the most sacred of Christian writings. The Gospels according to Matthew, Mark, Luke and John proclaim through dramatic narrative, recorded sayings and theological discourse the story of Jesus of Nazareth and the significance of His life, death and resurrection.

. . . Yet today, there are few Biblical scholars—from liberal skeptics to conservative evangelicals—who believe that Matthew, Mark, Luke and John actually wrote the gospels. Nowhere do the writers of the texts identify themselves by name or claim unambiguously to have known or traveled with Jesus. The majority of modern scholarly opinion holds that all four books were compiled from a variety of oral and written sources collected over a period of decades following Jesus' crucifixion, as the prologue to Luke suggests.

The Letters of Paul

Outside of Jesus himself, no one was more instrumental in the founding of Christianity than the Apostle Paul. . . . And if tradition is correct, he wrote nearly half of the New Testament: His letters to young churches in Greece, Rome and Asia Minor are among the earliest and most influential of Christian writings.

For most of Christian history, Paul's authorship of the thirteen letters bearing his name was widely accepted. But modern scholarship has raised serious questions, based on content as well as writing style, suggesting that some of the letters are pseudonymous—written by others who used Paul's name to lend them authority.

The Catholic Letters

Although Paul was the most prolific of New Testament writers, his were not the only letters that circulated among the far flung churches. As Christianity spread through the Roman Empire, other evangelists found the epistle an effective device for instructing and influencing the faithful. Seven letters, each with some claim to apostolic authorship, are included in the New Testament canon as "catholic" or universal epistles—so named because they appear to be written for general readership rather than to specific churches. While they bear the names of such central figures in the early church as James and Jude—believed by some to be brothers of Jesus—and the Apostles Peter and John, their authorship had been a subject of debate since the second century.

Another commentary on the New Testament was recently provided by a group of seventy-eight Bible scholars known as the "Jesus Seminar" in the book *The Five Gospels: The Search For The*

Authentic Words of Jesus.[10] Their judgment is that Jesus probably said only 18 percent of the words attributed to him in the five gospels (Matthew, Mark, Luke, John, and recently, Thomas) and, for example, that Jesus did not teach the Lord's prayer to his disciples, or predict that the world would end, or say "Drink from it, all of you," or control the wind and the waves, or raise Lazarus from the dead, or claim to be the messiah. The religion editor of the *St. Petersburg Times,* Thomas J. Billitteri, noted the conclusion of the scholars and their spokesman Robert W. Funk:

> The scholars dispute the authenticity of many of Jesus' sayings because he wrote nothing himself, because the Gospels vary dramatically in spots, and because they were written decades after his death.
>
> The gospel writers were not only disciples of Jesus, the scholars suggest, but skilled fiction writers who embellished Jesus' words with borrowed lore, passages from Greek scripture and other sources to fit the times and persuade their audiences that Jesus indeed was the long-awaited messiah.
>
> "The writers of the Gospels are really evangelists, not historians or biographers," Funk says. "So in a broad sense, we'd have to say the Gospels are really religious propaganda. What they are trying to do is make this figure (Jesus) a plausible candidate for the title of messiah or 'son of God' or 'son of man' or a figure who towers above similar charismatic miracle workers in the Hellenistic world."[11]

At the least, it seems apparent that many questions are still to be answered with respect to the origins and authorship of New Testament narratives. And there is no doubt that the Old Testament included a large measure of myth in its recountals. Certainly, neither the Old Testament nor the New Testament could be taken as authoritative in the sense intended by Saint Augustine, who believed that the Holy Ghost had vouchsafed the truth, accuracy, and authority of the Bible.

There is another perspective on holy books, however. They may be honored, if not for their scientific accuracy, then for the insights they provide on the development of human thought. Andrew Dickson White wrote this about science and holy scripture:

> Science, while conquering them, had found in our Scriptures a far nobler truth than that literal historical exactness for which theologians have so long and so vainly contended. More and more as we consider the results of the long struggle in this field we are brought to the conclusion that the inestimable value of the great sacred books of the world is found in their revelation of the steady striving of our race after higher conceptions, beliefs, and aspirations, both in morals and religion. Unfolding and exhibiting this long-continued effort, each of the great sacred books of the world is precious, and all, in the highest sense, are true. Not one of them, indeed, conforms to the measure of what mankind has now reached in historical and scientific truth; to make a claim to such conformity is folly, for it simply exposes those who make it and the books for which it is made to loss of their just influence.
>
> That to which the great sacred books of the world conform, and our own most of all, is the evolution of the highest conceptions, beliefs, and aspirations of our race from its childhood through the great turning-points in its history. Herein lies the truth of all bibles, and especially of our own. Of vast value they indeed often are as a record of historical outward fact; recent researches in the East are constantly increasing this value; but it is not for this that we prize them most: They are eminently precious, not as a record of outward fact, but as a mirror of the evolving heart, mind, and soul of man.[12]

As holy books embody "the deepest searchings into the most vital problems of humanity in all its stages: the naive guesses of the world's childhood, the opening conceptions of its youth, the more fully rounded beliefs of its maturity," they may be studied with profit. But with an understanding that history and myth are intermingled and that many of the stories are apocryphal. Wars, persecutions, and prejudices have all been justified—engendered—by statements in the Bible, just as Scripture has been the source of humanity's loftiest sentiments.

It is, then, significant that scholars now agree that holy books are subject to human error, or as George and Ira Gershwin put it:

> It ain't necessarily so,
> De t'ings dat yo' li'ble
> To read in de Bible,
> It ain't necessarily so.
> (*Porgy and Bess*)*

NOTES

1. Sir James Frazer, *Folklore in the Old Testament*, abridged ed. (New York: Avenel Books, 1988), p. 1.

2. Ibid., p. 2.

3. Ibid., p. 3.

4. Ibid., p. 4.

5. Ibid., p. 15.

---

6. Ibid., p. 45.

7. Ibid., p. 62.

8. Joseph Campbell, *Myths to Live By* (New York: Bantam Books, 1973), p. 24.

9. "Who Wrote the Bible?" *U.S. News & World Report,* December 10, 1990, p. 61.

10. Robert W. Funk and Roy W. Hoover, *The Five Gospels: The Search for the Authentic Words of Jesus* (New York: Macmillan Publishing Co., 1993).

11. Thomas J. Billitteri, *St. Petersburg Times,* January 29, 1994, p. 1.

12. Andrew Dickson White, *A History of the Warfare of Science with Technology in Christendom,* vol. 1 (New York: D. Appleton-Century, 1936), p. 22.

9

Magic:
Mere Wishful Thinking

agic was one way for humans to control their environment, religion was the other. Originally, magic was based on the premise that certain laws of nature controlled events in this world, quite independent of any gods or spirits. Religion was based on the premise that unseen spirits could override the laws of nature if it pleased them to do so.

From this standpoint, magic was very similar to science. Both assumed that, based on natural law, a given action would produce a predictable reaction. So a magician might sprinkle water on the ground believing that the natural consequence would be rain, just as the scientist might seed the clouds with the same expectation of rain. Neither technique involved calling on the spirits to perform a miracle.

Magic and science, then, were similar in their attempt to control nature by using nature's own laws. They differed in what they perceived these laws to be. And the obviously false premises of magic led it to become known as the "bastard sister of science." In all societies, however, science did not grow out of magic but simply pursued parallel uses and development.

INDIGENOUS MAGIC

The understanding of natural laws by indigenous peoples was based on their own observations, from which they drew two conclusions: first, that the effect usually resembles the cause and, second, that parts of the body may influence the whole. And from these conclusions came sympathetic magic of two types: imitative magic, where "like produces like," and contagious magic, where parts of the body may affect the whole, even when separated by time or space.

Imitative magic took many forms. There is the instance of a medicine man drawing the yellow jaundice from a patient by placing a yellow bird in his close proximity. Certain warriors around the world would not eat rabbit, believing that they might imitate the rabbit and develop a timid personality—for the same reason some tribes ate the meat of lions to develop a fearless character. Even the gods were chosen based on their perceived relation to the function performed; thus bulls or snakes were often worshiped as fertility gods and a yellow-haired goddess represented the corn crop.

Contagious magic was equally powerful in the mind of indigenes. So a magician could obtain a lock of hair from an enemy and by destroying the detached hair, destroy the enemy—without regard to the time or space which separated the magician from his victim. For this reason some tribes never cut their hair and some influentials paid retainers to eat their hair and nail clippings so they could not be appropriated by an enemy. Names were also carefully guarded in many indigenous societies, and fake identities given, so that magicians could not aim their curses with any degree of accuracy.

So both imitative and contagious magic were found throughout the primitive world. In its pure and unadulterated form, magic was not dependent on the spirit world for assistance. Indeed, in some cases both men and gods were believed subject to the same immutable laws of nature.

As magic became more sophisticated, professional magicians were employed to seek benefits for the entire community and they, in turn, expanded the possibilities of magic and heightened the prestige of the magician. The magician among indigenous peoples came to enjoy great stature in the community but of course operated under rather difficult circumstances: his calling was to produce rain, assure the harvest, heal the sick, destroy the enemy, and otherwise benefit the community—but there was no legitimacy to his modus operandi. He contrived, therefore, to gain as much real knowledge of the world as he might and use it for the common good, and to supplement his knowledge or theories with bold displays of confidence, impressive ceremonies and, perhaps, a frightening countenance or costume. In later days, many religions were similarly asked to perform miracles and likewise responded with the means at hand.

CIVILIZED MAGIC

As man progressed from primitive tribal societies to more advanced civilizations, magic remained an important element for controlling one's destiny and, if necessary, one's gods. In most cases, a belief in magic blended with a belief in the spirit world.

Some say that the religious beliefs of ancient Babylonia, for example, should more properly be called magic. Disease in Babylonia was attributed to the presence of evil spirits (which implies

Demon-King

Magicians claimed the ability to conjure up demons, this one a
bearded demon-king riding on a long-tailed dragon.

The British Museum. Michael Holford Photographs, England.

a religious belief) but was cured by transferring the disease to a doll-like image (which implies a belief in imitative magic).

Magic and religion commingled in Zoroastrianism, the religion of ancient Persia that profoundly influenced Jewish and Christian thought. One of the requirements of their magic was strict adherence to the magical rite; in purification rites, therefore, Zoroastrian priests cleansed the sinners with holy water or cow's urine sprinkled in strict sequence from head to left toe, which was the last refuge of demons.

Indian religions were host to many magical beliefs. In fact, the sacred books of India provide one of the best continuing records of the origin and evolution of magic. It was largely objections to the Hindu use of magic, and the attendant profiteering of Hindu priests, that led Buddhists to break away and form their own religion.

Ancient China was another country where magic was rampant. The wu were a class of sorcerers and witches who used the time-honored methods of encouraging the good spirits or expelling the evil spirits by dancing, chanting, beating drums, and going into ecstatic trances. Over time the wu magic was taken up by the Taoist religion. Then the Buddhist religion was obliged to compete with Taoist magic and did so in another time-honored tradition— by reporting an impressive series of miraculous occurrences.

Japanese magic was no less potent than other magic throughout the world, and like other magic it generally served very utilitarian purposes. One Shinto ritual was designed to discover the identity of the gods who had bungled all the crops in recent years. Another magic ritual used a horse whose erect ears, it was hoped, would encourage the gods to listen attentively.

Magic and religion also coexisted in ancient Egypt. The Egyptians treated their gods as humans and communicated with them on a regular basis. But when talk failed and threats, promises, and appeals were of no avail, the Egyptians returned to magic. In character, much of the Egyptian magic was derived from the principles of imitative magic and contagious magic. So there are examples of miniature hands to fight off evil spirits, miniature seals to contain evil spirits, and miniature crocodiles to devour evil spirits. A dwarf of clay would be placed on the forehead of a woman giving birth to assist in the delivery. As in Christian usage in later years, amulets, images, and beads were worn around the neck to protect or heal.

The Jews combined magic and religion in such a way as to maximize their utility. For example, the Jewish religion acknowledged the presence of demons but used magic to harness their evil energies for religious works; legend says that Solomon used evil spirits to assist in building the Temple in Jerusalem.[1] The connection between magic and religion was also apparent in that gifts and sacrifices were as common in Jewish magical rites as they were in Jewish religious rites.

So in most ancient civilizations the line between magic and religion was a thin one. The test in Egypt, and later in Greece and Rome, was one of orthodoxy, as defined by the state. Conventional practices were deemed to be religious, while unorthodox practices were classed as magic. In the interests of avoiding foreign incursions, the Roman government encouraged homegrown religions and the avoidance of foreign beliefs. However, the Roman citizenry was still attracted by the magic of foreign countries, particularly Egypt and Persia, because it was believed that the more ancient cultures had stronger magic, since they lived closer to the days of the gods.

ROMAN MAGIC

In Rome, anybody could be a magician, but the right education and training were important. An understanding of the forces of nature was of primary importance, and once a magician had established rapport with one aspect of the universe he was believed expert in all aspects—based again on principles of sympathetic magic. Some people had revelations from on high that opened up the secrets of the universe, and Maria the Jewess claimed to have been instructed by God himself.[2] Certain specialties, like prophecy, were thought to be particularly suited to women, and virginity was often required, based on the assumption that the seeress was married to the god she represented and that any infidelity might result in the loss of her god-given powers. Physical abnormalities or peculiarities surrounding one's birth could also lead to magical powers—a child of incest, for example, invariably possessed magical powers.

The timing of magical ceremonies was important, and sunrise, sunset, and phases of the moon were preferred, particularly a new moon and a full moon. The costumes were also set and called for a flowing white robe, possibly with purple streamers, or for the ceremony to be conducted in the nude. Purification rites were important in magic, as they were in religion.

Many different demons were called on for assistance and have gone on to become part of the language; for example, panic was caused by Pan. Some of the gods were exclusive to magic, but in most cases the gods called on by magic were the same as those used in religion. The complexity of the demoniac network grew and grew, until:

> the realm of the supernatural assumes more and more the aspect of an Oriental despotism with a thoroughly organized bureaucratic government, all in the hands of demons. There are secretaries, and undersecretaries, guards, doorkeepers, messengers—a regular hierarchy of demoniac officials, whose rank and functions are established and fixed with meticulous exactness.[3]

The greatest of all magicians was the goddess Hecate-Selene, queen of the ghosts, who "sweeps through the night followed by her dreadful train of questing spirits." Her power was altogether universal but her special demoniac talents dealt with the magic of love and metamorphosis.

The magic of ancient Greece and Rome was quite close to that of earlier peoples. Amulets were worn which could protect against demons. Small figures were fashioned from wax or clay to cast spells on a victim far removed. Jaundice could be transferred from a person to other living things that were colored yellow. To cure a stomach ache, the stomach of a frog could be pressed against the sufferer's belly and then discarded.

Magic served many functions: healing the sick, prolonging life, controlling the weather, assuring the harvest, restoring virility, and increasing sexual desire. Magic also provided protection from witches who took the form of screech owls to fly to their lover, but: "She never comes to him as a human or normal woman. The fires of hell are in her eyes, the fires of hell are in her veins, the taste of blood and death is on her lips. She is the erotic vampire, the succuba, as she was called in the Middle Ages—who haunts her victim in his dreams and little by little draws to herself the very marrow in his bones."[4]

Magic and religion shared many things. More often than not the gods were the same and the goals were the same. Magic and religion also shared another practice: to invoke the gods, or demons, with rites of sacrifice. And in keeping with the law of sympathetic magic, both magic and religion would sacrifice white doves to Aphrodite, fighting cocks to war gods, and black victims to the underworld as: "dark victims to the powers of darkness, light to the powers of light." So the ceremonies of magic and religion were essentially the same when Christianity emerged as the dominant religion.

CHRISTIANITY AND MAGIC

When Christianity became the state religion of the Roman Empire in the fourth century, Romans believed in very elementary forms of imitative and contagious magic. A Roman magician could raise the dead if he had a bone belonging to the deceased. A patient's jaundice could be transferred to a yellow bird. And Romans never ceased to believe that wheatears growing in a neighbor's field, while their own field did poorly, was a result of a magical transference of their crop; the practice was even forbidden by Roman law.

In most cases the gods, the ceremonies, and the sacrifices made in the name of Roman religion were the same as those made in the name of Roman magic. And if the early Christians opposed magic, they did not doubt its power; Christians saw the difference between their religion and magic as a difference between good and evil, but not as a difference between the real and the imaginary. So belief in a Christian God did not banish the pagan gods who were regarded as demons. Saint Augustine, for example, was quite certain that magical rites could be used to summon demons.

As Christianity spread, it was to have many confrontations with magic. Saint Patrick was said to have had real concerns about the magical powers of the Celtic women. Ireland became somewhat of a battleground with the magic of the evil druids matched, trick for trick, by the magic of the Christian saints—both parties changing shapes, rendering themselves invisible, producing food miraculously, and creating confusion by the power of their curses.

So, the Church believed in the power of magic. At first, the Church was to distinguish between black magic (to cause disease, natural disasters, and ill fortune) and white magic (to banish disease and bad weather and to predict the future), but eventually all forms of magic were classed together and attributed to Satan. And so it was believed that magic was the work of dethroned pagan gods who conspired against the Church and its constituents.

Witch-Finder

Matthew Hopkins was Witch-Finder General in England. His fees were based on extracting confessions, often from torturing the accused.

Mary Evans Picture Library, London.

In later centuries the Church acted with great force to ban magic, which by then had become somewhat confused with science:

- In 1163, Pope Alexander III forbade "the study of physics or the laws of the world" to all ecclesiastics who, at the time, were the only people in a position to attempt such studies.
- In 1231, Pope Gregory IX instituted the papal Inquisition to seek out heretics practicing alchemy, witchcraft, and sorcery (the use of torture to obtain confessions was authorized in 1252 by Innocent IV).
- In 1243, the Dominicans forbade members of the order the study of medicine and natural philosophy and in 1287 extended the prohibition to the study of chemistry.
- In 1317, Pope John XXII issued his bull *Spondent Pariter* which was aimed at alchemists but also hit the beginning studies of chemistry. Pope John noted that the lives of him and his followers were threatened by the arts of sorcerers who sent devils into mirrors, killed people with a magic word, and had tried to kill him by piercing a waxen image of him.
- In 1437 and 1445, Pope Eugene IV issued bulls encouraging inquisitors to seek out and punish magicians and witches who produce inclement weather.
- In 1484, Pope Innocent VIII issued his bull *Summis Desiderantes* which caused the death of tens of thousands of men, women, and children suspected of sorcery and magic. About this time the Church published the *Witch-Hammer, Malleus Maleficarum,* which was a manual detailing the means of detecting and punishing witches.
- The years 1504 and 1523 saw Pope Julius II and Pope Adrian VI issue similar bulls condemning magicians and witches.

Over the centuries, therefore, the leaders of Christianity have believed in magic. And the strength of their belief is documented both in written proclamations and by the death of those who were condemned for being sorcerers and witches—presumed to be possessed of magical powers that could be used against the Church and society at large. In this respect, the beliefs of the Christian priests have been no different from those of their counterparts in many religious cults whose priests are similarly committed to a belief in magic and magicians, such as the priests of voodoo.

Nor have we rid ourselves of a belief in magic to this day. Christians are still given to religious beliefs that are quite clearly based on sympathetic magic, the same magical beliefs that were held by the earliest societies. For example, the belief that body parts of the dead, when preserved, have powers to protect the living is true of current Catholic belief and was true thousands of years ago in various cults and cultures. And this is only one belief that demonstrates a continuing commitment to magic.

So from its beginning the Christian Church recognized magic as a real event and its belief in magic was confirmed many times throughout the centuries by virtue of the prohibitions issued by the popes and Protestant religious leaders. But magic was in fact nothing more than the wishful thinking of humans who were looking for ways to control their environment.

NOTE

1. James Hastings, ed., "Magic," *The Encyclopaedia of Religion and Ethics* (New York: Charles Scribner and Sons, 1951), p. 303.

2. Ibid., p. 281.

3. Ibid., p. 282.

4. Ibid., p. 280.

10

Prayer:
More Wishful Thinking

agic was the precursor to religion and played a significant role in the development of religious beliefs. Over the centuries, however, confidence in the power of magic lessened, presumably because of the erratic results. So humans looked for a new way of dealing with the spirits.

The alternative to magic was a softer and more persuasive approach to the spirit world—prayer. Genetically, prayer came from the spells and incantations of the magician and merely substituted a request for a command. Otherwise, however, there was not a great difference between magic and prayer. Sir James Frazer gives the example of the native viewing the drying lake bed and saying to the gods, "Oh, mighty spirit, do not let the fish hide in the mud." In addressing the gods in such a way, prayer and magic—request and command—were often indistinguishable.

Prayer took many turns. Some cultures began by bargaining with the gods for certain favors, but holding back a portion of their offerings until the gods gave proof of performance. The Japanese, through their emperor, rewarded the gods by promoting them to a higher grade or class for particularly meritorious service. The Egyptians modeled ears that were placed in their temples so the gods might hear from a distance. Some cultures punished the gods for nonperformance and many punished the priests or kings whose prayers did not prove effective. The ancient Hebrews were ordinarily very confident in their petitions and often gave thanks in advance; they also believed that people could and should ask for health, prosperity, and the good things in life.

Of course, traditions have evolved through the centuries and beliefs have been tempered by experience. Over time there were stages, or stair-steps, in attitudes toward prayer. At first, the gods were compelled to act by the power of magic. The next stage was a prayerful bargaining process of sorts and, following that, an appeal to reason. The final approach was an appeal to the sympathy of the gods, often undertaken from a submissive position. So from an attitude of approximate equality, humanity's later approach to the gods became one of humility.

As the approach to prayer evolved over the centuries, so did the idea of blame. In the earliest of times there was a tendency to blame poor results on the priest, or king, if he was the chosen mediator. The difficulty of the priest's position was clear, and after a number of painful losses in their ranks the ancient priests wisely shifted the burden of blame to the gods. The gods' neglect was then attributed to a capricious nature or to the opposition of malignant spirits. In either case, on occasion the gods themselves were punished and, if incorrigible, were replaced by more stable or more powerful deities. Eventually, however, both gods and priests were held blameless; today, the presumption is that the individual is often not worthy to receive favors from a god.

So prayer followed magic as another of humanity's attempts to control the environment—a way to assure the food supply, protect against natural disasters, and recover from injury and illness.

Ancient Supplicants

A group of worshipers with their hands clasped in the attitude of prayer, 3500 B.C.E.

The Oriental Institute of the University of Chicago.

BABYLONIAN

Several thousand years before Christ, the ancient Babylonians developed an extensive system of prayer combined at points with magical incantations. The prayer included private and public utterances, with long liturgies including choirs and responses between priest and laymen. One ritual that was later adapted by Christianity was the private confessional, which gave rise to penitential prayers to Marduk, sun-god and vegetation-god:

Choir:
Oh, lord, not wilt thou reject me, not, oh lord,
  wilt thou reject me.
Oh, lord, divine ram of heaven and earth,
  not wilt thou reject me.
Oh lord Marduk, not wilt thou reject me.[1]

Priest:
He that renders petition am I, thou wilt not reject me.
One of prayer am I, thou wilt not reject me.
One of intercession am I, thou wilt not reject me.[1]

During the earlier times in Babylonia, an afflicted person was thought to have been attacked by demons. Gradually, however, the priests assumed that the failure of the protective deity to take action must be due to sin on the part of the sufferer. In other words, the victim of illness must have done something to anger a god, which would explain why the priest's prayers were not being answered.

The idea that moral transgressions angered the gods, who in turn would not answer prayers, relieved both priest and god from fault and placed the blame on the shoulders of the penitent. Thus neither priest nor god could be accused of malingering or malignancy, and when the gods failed to act in time of need, the responsibility was in the laps of the people.

EGYPTIAN

Early Egyptian ritual contains many statements of address and adoration, as well as magic formulae, but there is little evidence of prayers of petition. In later times, personal prayers did ask the gods for protection and favors, and these were supposed to be more efficacious if done in silence as there was a value associated with secret prayer. In some cases, temples included models of human ears, positioned on stone slabs, so the gods could better hear the prayers of the faithful, even from a distance. One Egyptian prayer of the time said: "The goddess is a lion; she smiteth as a fierce lion smiteth and pursueth him that trespasseth against her. I cried to my mistress and found that she came to me with sweet breath. She was gracious to me after she had caused me to see her hand. She turned again to me in favour, she let me forget the sickness that was on me."[2]

GREEK

The ancient Greeks usually prayed for practical things: health, children, and success in business and war. The Greeks normally prayed aloud and louder still when important matters were at stake. There was silent prayer, however, on such occasions as when the prayer might be overheard by an enemy who conceivably could counteract the prayer with his own spell. Early Greek prayer began as a command to the gods, evolved into a bargaining process, and became much later a request not unlike that used today. An example of the rituals used was described in Jason's quest of the Golden Fleece:

> Now when that goodly crew were come to Iolkos, Jason mustered them with thanks to each, and the seer Mopsos prophesied by omens and by sacred lots, and with good will sped the host on board. And when they had hung the anchors over the prow, then their chief, taking in his hands a golden goblet, stood upon the stern and called on Zeus whose spear is the lightning, and on the tides of waves and winds and the nights, and the paths of the sea, to speed them quickly over, and for kindly days and the

friendly fortune of return. And from the clouds a favourable voice of thunder pealed in answer; and there came bright lightning flashes bursting through. Then the heroes took heart in obedience to the heavenly signs; and the seer bade them strike into the water with their oars, while he spake to them of happy hopes; and in their rapid hands the rowing sped untiringly. (Pind. Pyth. iv. 188 ff.)[3]

As often happened in ancient times, the prayers of Jason resulted in an immediate and miraculous response. It was usual for most enterprises, big or small, to begin by invoking the help of the gods.

HEBREW

After the long competition between Yahweh and Baal was resolved in favor of Yahweh, the Israelites placed great confidence in their God. The Old Testament reveals their commitment and their belief that Yahweh would always protect them and intervene in their behalf. In fact, so certain were the Israelites that their prayers would be answered that they frequently thanked Yahweh in advance. On occasion, some worshipers expressed anxiety and even disappointment, but the prevailing attitude was that prayers were sure to be answered. The Israelites asked for both spiritual and temporal blessings in full measure: long life, good health, and prosperous living conditions.

So from the beginning, prayer had been a part of Hebrew worship; sacrifice was the other. Prayer included utterances of thanksgiving, praise, petition, and confession, and could be directed to God without the use of intermediaries.

CHRISTIAN

Since Christianity began as a sect of Judaism, of course Christian prayer shared the same origins. Much of the early Christian liturgy is modeled on the Jewish, and the Lord's Prayer is made up of parts of the Jewish prayers.

Christianity preserved or extended the strong Jewish belief in the efficacy of prayer. The *New Catholic Encyclopedia* states the view:

> To the prayer of petition alone Our Lord has added the promise of infallible efficacy. "Amen, amen, I say to you, if you ask the Father anything in my name, he will give it to you. Hitherto you have not asked in my name. Ask, and you shall receive, that your joy may be full" (Jn 16:24; Mt 7.7, 21–22).[4]

The Catholic position adds that prayers will be infallibly fulfilled "not only for the just man but even for the sinner." There are conditions that must be met for efficacious prayer, however: devotion, attention, full confidence in God, and perseverance. To the extent that a prayer of petition represents an unusual opportunity, it is also a condition of salvation according to Catholic belief. Sacraments and meritorious works, alone, are not enough.

Other forms of Christian prayer include prayers of adoration, thanksgiving, and propitiation. Catholics and Protestants disagree on the question of sacraments and the intercession of saints, but are in general agreement on the ultimate power of prayer and paradoxically on the continuing presence of Satan, the supreme spirit of evil.

MUSLIM

Prayer is one of the "five pillars" of Muslim worship: (1) repetitions of the creed, (2) daily prayer, (3) almsgiving, (4) fasting, and (5) pilgrimage to Mecca. The Muslim is required to visit a mosque on Friday of each week and join in prayers led by an imam, who is a pious member of the community. On other days the Muslim is required to pray at five appointed times, and either by tape recorder or a muezzin the faithful are called to pray:

> "God is most great" (this is said four times); "I testify that there is no God but Allah" (twice); "I testify that Muhammad is Allah's apostle" (twice); "Come to prayer" (twice); "Come to security" (twice); "God is most great" (twice); "There is no God but Allah."

In the beginning Muhammad turned toward Jerusalem during daily prayers, but a quarrel with the Jews in Medina led to facing toward Mecca. The Muslim law prescribes in detail how prayers must be performed, the position of the body, the direction to be faced, purification proceedings, and the appropriate coverings for the body. Stipulations on covering the body may have originated as protection against demons who were supposed to be present at prayer time; thus women covered their bodies except face and hands and men their heads and at least the part between waist and knees. On Friday of each week the communal prayers are held in a mosque. Whether prayer is said alone or in a group, it is not an individual communication or appeal to God. Prayer is a ritual recognition of Allah; it is not said to secure favors for the individual worshiper.

HINDU

Hinduism embraces a broad range of religious beliefs and in that diversity prayer, as commonly defined, is difficult to identify. To achieve Nirvana, a deliverance from the cycle of rebirth, a person may use: devotion to the gods, asceticism, meditation, and obedience to the rules of caste. To receive forgiveness for sins, a person may make: payments to a priest, pilgrimages to a shrine, devotions to a god, repetitions of a god's name, and visits to sacred places such as the Ganges where sins may be washed away. So, many options are at hand for the worshiper. Also available to the individual is the Atharva-Veda, a sacred book containing prayers and rituals for the home, together with spells and incantations to drive off evil spirits.

JAINIST

In the sixth century B.C.E., Jainism, like Buddhism, rejected the sacrificial approach of Hinduism to achieving release from the cycle of reincarnation. Again like Buddhists, Jainists believed that release from life was achieved by an individual's accomplishments. In this belief, there was very little role for the more conventional form of prayer.

- Petition: Jainists believe that a previous life affects the current existence. One's happiness, unhappiness, wealth, or poverty is a result of one's good or bad actions in a past life. Petitioning the gods for favors would be inappropriate under this system.
- Intercession: On the same basis, it would be inappropriate and ineffectual to intercede for another person, who is being

rewarded or punished for a prior life. Such intercession would itself be considered the sin of bribery.

- Adoration: Adoration is an element of prayer allowed Jainists, but it is more in the nature of tribute than an emotional encounter.
- Thanksgiving: The Jainist cannot give thanks as he has neither asked for nor received favors. His own past actions explain his current condition.
- Confession: Confession is encouraged, but not as a way to obtain forgiveness of sins. The penance given by the director, however, may mitigate the transgression somewhat.

Temple worship is an important part of Jainist worship and requires a complex ritual. Special clothes, movements, utterances, incense, and offerings are all required in a ceremony to bathe and feed the idols of the gods. The worshiper strikes a gong when he is finished.

BUDDHIST

Buddhism, which also began before 500 B.C.E., also has a very different concept of prayer from its Hindu forebear. In fact, Buddhists do not believe in prayer in the form of a petition to a god. Their belief is that everyone is personally responsible for reaching a state of religious perfection and that no help is coming from a supreme being. In his lifetime, Buddha was careful not to seek specific favors from any gods. After his death, however, he was himself so revered that he became a model and a master, and his followers vowed to attain a similar state of perfection. In some respects, these vows could be considered prayers, but they represent statements of purpose and conviction, not of petition.

SHINTO

The primitive Japanese had very little experience with personal prayer. The early Mikados, however, would offer prayer on behalf of all the people. These prayers were offered to a number of gods, including some of the departed Mikados, but they differed from the concept of Western prayer. The object of Japanese prayer was less concerned with moral progress and a spiritual high road than with getting help with the weather, the crops, epidemics, and earthquakes. The emperor and his protection were also the subject of many ritual prayers. In addition to Shinto prayers of petition and some of expiation, the Mikado used prayer as a means of communication, on occasion announcing some important piece of news to the gods—an accession to the throne, the changing of the name of an era, an enemy invasion. The most interesting among these announcements are unquestionably those advising a deity of his promotion, by the emperor, to a higher rank in the celestial hierarchy. The *Encyclopaedia of Religion and Ethics* notes:

> In 672 three deities supplied some useful military information; as soon as the war was finished, the emperor, upon the report received from his generals, raised these deities to a higher rank. In 838 a similar distinction was bestowed on a young god in defiance of seniority, and a jealous goddess showed her anger by pouring a volcanic shower on the eastern provinces. In 840 the great deity of Deha sent a shower of stones, and the emperor conferred the second grade of the fourth rank on her, with congratulations on her marvelous power. In 851 Susa-no-wo and Oho-kuni-nushi obtained the second grade of the third rank, and, eight years after, the first grade of the same rank, which, however, does not make them higher than an important minister or a successful chamberlain. In 860 a volcano of Satsuma was placed in a lower subdivision of the second grade of the fourth rank. In 868 the gods of Hirota and Ikuta caused seismic

shocks, and were immediately presented with a diploma. In 898, 340 gods were promoted by the emperor Daigo as a bounty, at his happy accession. In 1076 and 1172 promotions were made "en masse."[5]

Shinto prayer was often more inclined to bargain with the gods than to beg. Gifts and compliments would be extended in return for expected favors, but some offerings might be withheld pending proof of satisfactory performance. It was not necessarily in the nature of the Japanese to trust the gods implicitly which, in the Christian religion, is essential to the success of the prayer.

TIBETAN

By all odds, the Tibetans are the people most dedicated to prayer. This devotion has been attributed to the isolation of their country and to the extreme weather conditions which, perhaps under-standably, foster prayers of petition. The Tibetans invoke both the human and the celestial Buddhas of Mahayana Buddhism, but a number of gods are also available for assistance. There are also innumerable earth-demons, many of whom were imported from India. The earth-demons are under the authority of a goddess called the Grandmother of Ghosts, who dresses in yellow robes, carries a golden noose, and rides on a ram.

A feature of Tibetan prayer, like Christian prayer, is the rosary and a belief in the efficacy of repetition. Tibetan beads number 108 and are made from such diverse materials as conch shells, crystals, seeds, stones, and human skulls. Tibetans have also made extensive use of prayer flags and prayer wheels. The flags are nothing more than inscriptions, usually astrological in nature, that are raised on tall masts near temples or shrines. The prayer wheel extends the idea of repetition by printing thousands of prayers on a long strip of paper which is then coiled inside a prayer wheel. The wheel is then spun and the spinner credited with the prayers passed in each rotation.

Prayer wheels have been used in other societies as well. Some are called "wheels of fortune" and may be turned after a nominal payment to the priest. The Japanese, Egyptian, and Greek religions all used prayer wheels at points in their history, as has the English church. The prayer wheels containing texts have ranged from smaller, handheld wheels for personal use to the larger institutional sizes favored by lamaseries. Travelers in the East have described prayer wheels the size of barrels, lined up as in a beer cellar and requiring several people to set in motion. One monastery is reported to inventory one hundred large bobbins, each containing ten thousand invocations, so that in a few minutes the worshiper can achieve revolutions that are the equivalent to one million prayers.

So there were, and are, fundamental differences around the world with respect to asking for help from the gods. The differences range from total disbelief that a spirit world dispenses favors to a conviction that all wishes will be answered. A belief in prayers of petition, then, has not been a universal experience, but a matter of teaching and tradition.

It may be observed that in religions that do not believe in prayers of petition as such, the faithful are sustained by the promise of a better tomorrow—that another life or incarnation will more than make up for the deficiencies of this life. So in that sense, all prayer reflects the hope that some personal advantage may be gained by the supplicant, either immediately or in another existence. Those expecting temporal rewards, as opposed to eternal, are obviously more apt to know disappointment, although disappointment has not necessarily dampened the Christian enthusiasm for prayers of petition.

The explanation for the continuing Christian belief in prayer is once again wishful thinking, which has proven strong enough to overcome the clear evidence that humans are not able to call down health, wealth, and happiness for themselves and others at will. And strong enough also to ignore the illogic of a Christian resource which enables members to secure advantages which are not available to non-Christian segments of the world's population—which would be a most unchristian concept to acknowledge. So the power of human wishes, with the encouragement of the clergy, has blocked out the palpable objections to the idea that all is possible through prayer and that we need only ask and shall certainly receive.

It does appear, nevertheless, that science has replaced prayer where it was able to offer a viable and demonstrable solution to a problem and thus prayer has become less of a factor in our everyday lives. Other techniques to control the gods, such as magic and sacrifice, are also less a part of our lives although there are vestigial remains.

Finally, prayer in all its forms—petition, thanksgiving, adoration—is an imaginative attempt to establish rapport with the gods and by doing so to gain a measure of control over them. But prayer may also serve a social purpose, by enabling the supplicant to establish a relationship with his or her god, who cannot be seen, heard, or experienced in any way other than through prayer. As a communication, prayer may reflect the natural desire of men and women to relate socially, intimately, to other beings even when they are gods. The gods, then, are silent, unseen companions who accompany us through life, satisfy a human need for togetherness, and take on a reality of their own as the object of our prayers. And so prayer becomes another amazing invention of the human mind.

NOTES

1. James Hastings, ed., "Prayer," *The Encyclopaedia of Religion and Ethics* (New York: Charles Scribner and Sons), p. 159.

2. Ibid., p. 163.

3. Ibid., pp. 181, 185.

4. "Prayer," *The New Catholic Encyclopedia,* p. 671.

5. Hastings, "Prayer," *The Encyclopaedia of Religion and Ethics,* p. 190.

11

Sacrifice:
A Gift to the Gods

hen early peoples sought alternatives to magic, they turned to prayer and sacrifice as the means to control the gods. Prayer was essentially entreaty, sacrifice an offering of value. Both were perceived as pleasing to the gods, a judgment no doubt based on experience in dealing with human beings.

Sacrifice served many purposes in the lives of ancient peoples. It was used to appease the gods, to atone for sins and allay guilt, to secure advantage for one's self and one's community, and even to serve as a ransom paid to a devil—for the ancients were obliged to deal with the evil spirits as well as the good. The offering took many forms, but its value was often related to the importance of the request or occasion. And so it happened that human life was often placed on the altar, as it were, and even the life of one's child.

Some scholars believe that human sacrifice as such may have begun with cannibalism that subsequently took on religious overtones. Other scholars speculate that earlier humans saw death all around them, supposed that spirits were calling for these deaths, and decided that it was better to satisfy the appetite of the gods with somebody else—a survival strategy.

Over the centuries, blood sacrifices included both humans and animals, the animals offered either as food for the gods or simply as valuable gifts. It was many centuries later when the Greeks and other ancient cultures began to see a moral weakness in blood offerings even of an animal victim.

Perhaps they also began to doubt the efficacy of the sacrificial rite, just as the efficacy of magic must have come under question in earlier times. Finally blood sacrifices were abandoned, although many living religions, including Christianity, have chosen to recall the concept of human and animal sacrifice and represent it symbolically in their current rituals.

HUMAN SACRIFICE

The concept of human sacrifice began among indigenous peoples. In West Africa, natives asked the king to stop excessive rain by making juju—a sacrifice. A woman was made ready by prayer and a message to the rain-god put in her mouth. She was then clubbed to death and put in a high tree so the rain could see. A charm for bringing rain was to lash a young woman to a scaffolding placed high in a tree where she would be devoured by turkey buzzards. Similar rites were available for assuring a good harvest or controlling the sun.

The ancient Mexicans thought of the sun as a vital life force and named him Ipalnemohuani, or "He by whom all men live." As the Mexicans believed the sun gave life to the world, they believed he needed to receive life from it. And since the heart was the symbol of human life, the bleeding hearts of men were offered to the sun to give him strength to continue his journey across the sky. *The Golden Bough* notes:

The constant demand for human victims to feed the solar fire
was met by waging war every year on the neighboring tribes and
bringing back troops of natives to be sacrificed on the altar.
Thus the ceaseless wars of the Mexicans and their cruel system
of human sacrifices, the most monstrous on record, sprang in
great measure from a mistaken theory of the solar system.[1]

Scholars estimate that between twenty thousand and forty
thousand people a year were sacrificed in Mexico. Other cultures
believed the sun drove a horse-drawn chariot across the sky, so
they sacrificed horses, not men, to help the sun along. The ancient
Greeks, the kings of Judah, Spartans, and Persians all sacrificed
horses to the sun, and some drove the chariots off a cliff as well.

Second only to the Mexicans, perhaps, were the Indian sacrifices
to the dreaded goddess Kali. In some temples a human victim was
sacrificed to Kali every Friday evening. The victim was generally purchased for the purpose, although this was not always possible. Frequently, therefore, the victim was a person who had been kidnapped
from a neighboring village, or a traveler who was passing through or
simply some person who was found wandering the streets after mid-
night. When the British ruled India, the Friday night ceremony was
altered, at British request, and a sheep was substituted. As recently as
the beginning of the twentieth century it was believed that human sacrifices were still offered to Kali, on occasion, by almost every district
in India. Poison, mass immolation, and decapitation were all in use.

Human sacrifices were more than bloody gifts to the gods. On
some occasions, or in some cultures, sacrifices were made to
establish a communion with the gods. In other cases the religious
spirit became cannibalism and the victims were eaten. At times,
sacrifice also satisfied a public desire for spectacle, as did the
gladiator games of Rome or the massacres in Mexico. The public
spectacle of capital punishment in England also may have satisfied a deep-seated need for aggression.

Human sacrifices were also used for atonement and to benefit a particular individual. The practice of parents sacrificing the firstborn child was found in ancient Semitic religion and in Australia, China, America, Africa, and Russia. The death of Christ was conceived of as the sacrifice of a god-man for the atonement of human sins, although Westermarck notes that "the Greek Church and the most important of the Western Fathers regarded the death of Christ as a ransom for mankind paid to the devil."[2]

In summary, the act of human sacrifice is explained by Westermarck: "When men offer the lives of their fellowmen in sacrifice to their gods, they do so, as a rule, in the hopes of thereby saving their own."[3] He describes it as a form of life insurance and not so much an act of wanton cruelty as an absurdity.

KINGLY SACRIFICES

Even the king, or especially the king, was at risk in certain primitive societies. The king was viewed as a man-god and responsible for the welfare of his people. Therefore, if the king grew long in the tooth and showed signs of decay, it was a clear threat to the welfare of his people. The answer was to be found in replacing the king with a strong successor and allowing the king's soul to change bodies before it became impaired by the decay.

On a timely basis, therefore, the king would be sacrificed for the greater good. There are many examples, some rather poignant. In one society the decay of the king was measured by his incapacity to satisfy the sexual passion of his wives, who were numerous. *The Golden Bough* reports "when this ominous weakness manifested itself, the wives report it to the chiefs . . . and he is strangled in a hut which has been specially built for the occasion." All in all, the attitude toward the king was one of great respect and regicide was the final proof of his popular regard.

With understandable enterprise, a number of kings provided temporary royalty for sacrifice in their stead. A shah of Persia was known to have abdicated the throne, crowned a new king, and, following the execution of the temporary king three days later, reascended the throne. The decree of the stars had been fulfilled by the sacrifice.

In another situation, a line of Ethiopian kings willingly followed the mandates of the priests who, at will, could advise the king that his time had come as the gods required his sacrifice. The kings obeyed down to the reign of a monarch who, benefiting from a Greek education, questioned the thinking of the priests. The king solved this philosophical dilemma by entering the Golden Temple with a handful of soldiers and putting the priests to the sword.

In some societies it was customary for a king to provide his son for sacrifice. Ancient Semitic kings were not alone in sacrificing their sons as a ransom to the avenging demons. According to tradition, On, king of Sweden, sacrificed nine of his sons to the god Odin in order that his own life might be spared. *The Golden Bough* notes that Odin required one son to be sacrificed every nine years in order for the king to preserve his life. The Swedes stopped the monarch just before he dispatched his tenth, and last, son to Odin.

So, the importance of kings often led to their sacrifice. People became concerned when their king, frequently revered as a man-god, showed signs of weakness or decay. In some African societies the appearance of wrinkles, gray hair, or a missing tooth could be a convincing sign of decay in a man-god. On the other hand, kings shared many of the same superstitions and went to some lengths to arrange for a sacrifice that would at once satisfy the gods and preserve their own existence.

Abraham's Sacrifice

A copper circumcision plate shows Abraham about to sacrifice his son Isaac, as a winged angel hovers overhead. Dated 1653.

The Jewish Museum/Art Resource, New York City.

BIBLICAL SACRIFICES

The Book of Genesis says that God ordered Abraham to sacrifice his son as a burnt offering. As he said: "Take now thy son, thine only son Isaac, whom thou lovest, and get thee into the land of Moriah; and offer him there for a burnt offering upon one of the mountains which I will tell thee of" (Gen. 22:2, 9, 10).

The proposed sacrifice of Isaac was stopped by an angel and a ram was sacrificed in his place. The biblical suggestion of burnt offerings, nevertheless, describes an attitude toward child sacrifice and suggests that the patriarchs may have practiced human sacrifices in previous times.

History provides some background for the biblical references. Among the ancient Semites, kings were sometimes known to sacrifice their sons, particularly in times of national crisis. *The Golden Bough* quotes Philo of Byblus, whose work on the Jews says: "It was an ancient custom in a crisis of great danger that the ruler of a city or nation should give his beloved son to die for the whole people, as a ransom offered to the avenging demons; and the children thus offered were slain with mystic rites. So Cronus, whom the Phoenicians call Israel, being king of the land and having an only-begotten son called Jeoud (for in the Phoenician tongue Jeoud signifies 'only begotten'), dressed him in royal robes and sacrificed him upon an altar in a time of war, when the country was in great danger from the enemy" (p. 340). In a similar example, when the king of Moab was besieged by the Israelites, he offered his eldest son as a burnt sacrifice on the wall of the city.

History also provides a graphic description of infant sacrifice, referred to in the Bible as "making them pass through the fire." *The Golden Bough* describes a ceremony in ancient Carthage:

> a bronze image of the sun represented as a man with a bull's head. In order to renew the solar fires, human victims may have been sacrificed to the idol by being roasted in its hollow body or placed on its sloping hands and allowed to roll into a pit of fire. It was in the latter fashion that the Carthaginians sacrificed their offering to Molech. The children were laid on the hands of a calf-headed image of bronze, from which they slid into a fiery oven, while the people danced to the music of the flutes and timbrels to drown out the shrieks of the burning victims. The resemblance which the Cretan traditions bear to the Carthaginian practice suggests that the worship associated with the names

of Minos and the Minotaur may have been powerfully influenced by that of a Semitic Baal. (p. 326)

The biblical story of Jepthah's daughter is another example of child sacrifice. The spirit of the Lord was supposed to come upon Jepthah and, in return for help in defeating his enemies, he offered a vow to the Lord: "If thou shall without fail deliver the children of Ammon into mine hands, then it shall be that whatsoever cometh forth of the doors of my house to meet me, when I return in peace from the children of Ammon, shall surely be the Lord's, and I will offer it up for a burnt offering" (Judg. 11:30–31).

Jepthah fought the battle and won. He returned home and his daughter, an only child, came out to meet him. Jepthah kept his vow and sacrificed his daughter as a burnt offering. There are other indications in the Old Testament that children were at one time sacrificed. Leviticus warned against infant sacrifice: "You shall not surrender any of your children to Molech" (Lev. 18:21). The words of Micah suggested that child sacrifice was no longer necessary, nor sacrifice of any sort:

> With what shall I come before the Lord,
>   and bow myself before God on high?
> Shall I come before him with burnt offerings,
>   with calves a year old?
> Will the Lord be pleased with thousands of rams,
>   with ten thousands of rivers of oil?
> Shall I give my first-born for my transgression,
>   the fruit of my body for the sin of my soul?
> He has showed you, O man, what is good;
>   and what does the Lord require of you but to do justice,
>   and love kindness, and to walk humbly with your God.
>   (Mic. 6:6–8)

FIRSTBORN

The very early tribes believed that the firstfruits of the season belonged to a deity and were his due, or that the god or spirit actually inhabited the firstfruits. Whichever the case, it was thought politic to conduct a ceremony of thanksgiving before eating the firstfruits, which were then partaken of sacramentally or offered to the god. Some Brazilian Indians, for example, would not eat the new maize until their medicine man had danced and shouted his way into a trance, then bit the husk and blessed all concerned.

The value placed on the firstfruits of the season was later associated with the firstborn of animals and humans. Some tribes believed that firstborn children possessed unusual powers such as the ability to stop excessive rain or prevent dust storms. Other tribes were so proud of their firstborn that the parents assumed the name of the child. But many tribes regarded the firstborn child as the most valuable gift that could be offered to their god—and therefore sacrificed the child to gain the favor of the god.

Among the cultures that sacrificed the firstborn child were the ancient Celtics, Russians, and Semites. The ancient Semitic people, for example, believed that the blood of their forebears ran strongest in the firstborn, which made those children an especially valuable offering. And since the firstborn was the first gift of God after marriage, the child was in a sense still God's property—and therefore was sometimes returned to God as a burnt offering. It is uncertain whether such sacrifices were done on a regular basis or represented an unusual situation which called for an extraordinary sacrifice.

The Hebrew prophets came to denounce the sacrifice of the firstborn as a heathen practice. As a result, the Book of the Covenant stipulated that firstborn children need not be sacrificed if redeemed by the payment of a fee to the priest—a tradition of redemption that has been continued to this day.

Other methods of redemption included the Muhammadan

practice of sacrificing a goat or ram in place of the child. Some cultures offered effigies instead of the child, including a coconut because in appearance it resembled a human head.

SCAPEGOATS

Sacrifice has also been involved in the use of scapegoats. In this instance people have assumed that their pain or guilt could be transferred to another person, or animal, who would suffer in their place. This concept began when the low intellectual level of many early cultures caused people to think they could shift a burden of sorrow or guilt to another being just as they might shift a load of wood to another carrier—a simple failure to differentiate between the mental and the physical, the material and the spiritual.

In ancient Arabia, for example, a camel would be walked through a town struck with pestilence so that it could absorb the disease; the camel was then strangled with the assumption that the pestilence died with the beast. In certain African tribes, monkeys or rats were paraded through the village to attract evil spirits and then crucified to save the entire community from demonic attacks.

Scapegoats included divine animals and divine men. For example, Jewish high priests laid hands on the head of a goat to transfer the sins of the children of Israel to the goat, which was then banished into the wilderness. The ancient Aztecs believed that the sacrifice of a man-god absolved them of their sins. Similarly, Christians came to believe that they were absolved from sin by Christ, whose death was a redemption.

The transference of sin, then, is a concept which persists to this day, although its origin was in the magic of early humans. There are other examples where the principles of sympathetic magic found their way from primitive beliefs to religious doctrine of great sophistication.

CHRISTIAN SACRIFICE

The followers of Christ chose to regard his execution at the hands of the Roman authorities as a sacrifice and, as such, his death was thus glorified in subsequent accounts. Even among his followers, however, there was considerable debate on the nature of the sacrificial act.

The Christian religion now explains the death of Christ as a redemption of humans from primal, or original, sin. The theory of primal sin, however, did not begin with Christianity, but with the Orphic movement in ancient Greece, near the fifth century B.C.E. Orpheus was a mythical Greek hero endowed with superhuman musical abilities whose adventures included charming Hades, king of the underworld, and the mythical guardians of the River Styx. He came to an unfortunate end by dismemberment at the urging of rival gods, although "his head, still singing, with his lyre, floated to Lesbos, where an oracle of Orpheus was established."[4] The head continued to prophesy until a jealous Apollo ordered his dismembered limbs gathered up and buried; his lyre became a constellation in the heavens. From this beginning, and subsequently in the philosophic schools of ancient Greece, was born a mystic Greek religion which offered to purify the soul from innate evil. Christianity later adopted the concept of primal sin and linked it to the death of Christ, whose death then became purposeful—a sacrifice that would redeem the human race from primal sin. The concept began, nevertheless, with a mythical musician whose singing and dancing were "so beautiful that animals and even trees and rocks moved about him in dance."

The concept of original sin was a curious one, and certainly not an attractive one on the face of it, but it found acceptance among the Christian faithful. One reason is that the death of Christ was thereby exalted, transformed from the unremarkable execution of a political agitator into a holy sacrifice that would save humankind for all time to come. The concept of primal sin was important also, in that it explained the suffering that blanketed a world supposedly under the protection of a capable and caring God. With original sin, the blame for all natural disasters and human misfortunes shifted from God to human and the Creator was absolved of any responsibility.

Certainly the Jewish people were perplexed as to why their Yahweh would rain disaster on his chosen people, in a seemingly endless stream. And, perhaps fittingly, it was a Jew, Saul of Tarsus, whose Roman name was Paul, who first preached the doctrines of original sin and salvation through the sacrificial death of Christ. The idea of original sin was not explicitly mentioned in the Old Testament and in the New Testament it was Paul who alluded to the transmission of hereditary guilt from the first man to the entire human race. The *New Catholic Encyclopedia* notes:

> While one may gather, here and there in the NT, hints at the universality of sin, it is only St. Paul, in Eph 2.3 ("We were by nature children of wrath even as the rest") and especially in Rom 5.12–19, who forcefully brings out the doctrine. Through an extended series of contrasts Paul's doctrine gains great power: sin and death have entered into all men (Rom 5.12); in the transgression of the one, the rest died (5.15); consequent upon the judgment passed on one man, all men were condemned (5.18); and through the disobedience of one man the rest were constituted sinners (5.19).[5]

Freud saw a sense of original sin, or guilt, arising from a primordial act of murder, wherein the sons ordinarily acted to displace the primeval father in order to gain the sexual privileges and other preferments of his position. Today's biologists would reject the idea that characteristics acquired in a primordial setting could be genetically handed down for generations. The well-known

Oedipus complex, however, as a fantasy or neurosis might engender feelings of guilt and help to explain the acceptance of original sin as a concept and the need for expiation through sacrifice. Freud's comments in *Moses and Monotheism* offer an interesting perspective:

> Original sin and salvation through sacrificial death became the basis of the new religion founded by Paul. The question whether there was a leader and instigator to the murder among the horde of brothers who rebelled against the primeval father, or whether that figure was created later by poets who identified themselves with the hero and was then incorporated into tradition, must remain unanswered. After the Christian doctrine had burst the confines of Judaism, it absorbed constituents from many other sources, renounced many features of pure monotheism, and adopted in many particulars the ritual of the other Mediterranean peoples. It was as if Egypt had come to wreak her vengeance on the heirs of Ikhnaton. The way in which the new religion came to terms with the ancient ambivalency in the father-son relationship is noteworthy. Its main doctrine, to be sure, was the reconciliation with God the Father, the expiation of the crime committed against him; but the other side of the relationship manifested itself in the Son, who had taken the guilt on his shoulders, becoming God himself beside the Father and in truth in place of the Father. Originally a Father religion, Christianity became a Son religion. The fate of having to displace the Father it could not escape.[6]

Through the ages, then, the concept of religious sacrifice has taken many turns. Certainly there was a logic of sorts in offering a gift to those beings who were thought to control the universe as well as one's own affairs, although we may wonder at the logic of a powerful sun-god who yet needs human hearts to fuel his movements, of a benevolent god who calls for the sacrifice of children, or an almighty god who demands atonement from his own creations. But neither reasonableness nor proof of performance were required as a basis for sacrifice. The rite of sacrifice was based on a simple evaluation of what an unseen spirit, of good or evil intent, might fancy as an offering. And the clergy must have taken their own proclivities into account, for spirits have not forwarded a wish list to guide the decision. From this standpoint, the nature of the sacrifice may offer some insights into the character of the clergy, if not the culture overall. And perhaps the abandonment of blood sacrifices, human or animal, marks some growth in the religious outlook over the centuries and in civilization.

The theme of blood sacrifices, however, has remained in many living religions, including the Christian religion. It is an interesting occurrence that, even in our century, the sacrificial rites of indigenous peoples may be viewed as bizarre and repugnant, and yet the debt that our Christianity owes to these same ancient concepts is unmistakable.

NOTES

1. Sir James G. Frazer, *The Golden Bough,* abridged ed. (New York: Macmillan Publishing Co., 1922), p. 91.

2. James Hastings, ed., "Human Sacrifice," *The Encyclopaedia of Religion and Ethics* (New York: Charles Scribner and Sons, 1951), p. 842.

3. Ibid.

4. *Encyclopaedia Britannica,* s.v. "Orpheus."

5. "Original Sin," *New Catholic Encyclopedia* (New York: McGraw-Hill, 1967), p. 777.

6. Sigmund Freud, *Moses and Monotheism* (New York: Vintage Books, 1967), p. 175.

12

Miracles:
About Walking on Water

The gods of old were chosen for their powers to control the elements and protect their followers—and when they did not they were apt to be replaced by other gods. So claims of miraculous powers for a god were to be expected as well as the enthusiastic support of the claims by his priests and prophets. It was by definition, then, that a god performed miracles and thereby gained the acceptance of the people. Godhood could scarcely be claimed without miraculous powers.

So as the godlike figures of the world were introduced, their arrival was accompanied by reports of miraculous powers, whether or not they personally lay claim to such distinction. For example, a display of heavenly lights often provided a poetic accompaniment to the approach of godlike figures and also suggested a direct link between them and the creator of the universe; thus the sacred books of India recount that the births of Krishna and Buddha were announced by heavenly lights, while stars and meteors also marked the arrival of Yu, Lao-tzu, Moses, Abraham, various Caesars, and Christ.

Actually, the birth of the great ethnic teachers was said to be surrounded by many marvelous circumstances—heavenly lights were only the beginning. Typically: "The moment of birth is hailed by a great variety of portents on earth, in the sky, or in the lower regions. Unearthly lights are seen, mysterious music is heard. Prophecies of future greatness are made. The child himself speaks, laughs, stands, walks, or announces his intention of saving the world. Or, again, the child is miraculously saved from persecution and danger of death. There are also wonderful signs at the death of some ethnic teachers, especially at Buddha's death."[1]

Many of these same religious founders made no personal claim to miraculous powers and often were on record against the presumption of miracles. Confucius was said to be indifferent to spiritual concerns and avoided dealing with the supernatural and is quoted: "to search for what is mysterious, and practice marvelous arts, in order to be mentioned with honour in future ages—this is what I do not do." Muhammad disliked the idea of miracles and spoke of none on his own behalf. Lao-tsu was a humble teacher and opposed magic and the miraculous. Buddha protested against miracles and suspected they were wrought to convert people to the faith, saying, "I command my disciples not to work miracles."

After Buddha's death, nevertheless, his followers assigned a number of miracles to him, including healing wounds, making flood waters recede, treading on top of water or passing miraculously over it, and walking through a wall. Finally, Buddha was given the status of a man-god.

Frequently, as well, the godlike figure was said to be born of a virgin and with the ability to return from the dead. Joseph Campbell noted that: "Modern scholarship, systematically comparing the myths and rites of mankind, has found just about everywhere legends of virgins giving birth to heroes who die and are resurrected."[2] In addition to the miraculous circumstances of these comings (and goings), the god in question was obliged to demonstrate other spectacular powers that would at once set him apart from mortal men and women and above the gods of other religions.

Just as the godlike figures were often associated with miracles, many of the lesser figures of the religion were thought to have extraordinary powers, and frequently the same miracles were seen in different religions:

> In most of these religions miracles are commonly attributed to saints, sages, and ascetics. They bear a similar character in widely distant regions and under different creeds, and often run on parallel lines. Here again these miracles bear a curious likeness to many which are ascribed to Christian saints. Taoist, Zoroastrian, Buddhist, Hindu, and Muhammadan all believe in the possibility of the miraculous in the case of gifted persons. In Taoism those who through asceticism and saintliness "rise to the Tao" become like gods and are superior to the laws of nature. In Buddhism the cause is profound meditation. By this the *arhat* gains transcendent faculties—the five *abhijñas* ("magical posers") and *iddhi*, saintship, but also the power of working miracles. Holy men in Islam possess similar powers as a result of their faith, piety, and self-denial. They are also helped to them by the jinn and by knowledge of the divine name. The range of these wonders in the different religions is very wide. It includes a great variety of powers over nature—the production or cessation of storms or sunshine, causing the sun to stand still, drinking up rivers, superiority to fire or water (e.g., not being wet in heavy showers, or walking or passing through water); superiority to the limitations of matter and space (a common Buddhist attribute), the power of invisibility, change of form or of sex, invulnerability, levitation and swift passage through space, penetrating walls, mountains, earth, lengthening beams of wood, opening doors without keys, swift transference from one

Healing Gods

The principal healing god of antiquity, Asclepios, with his sacred snake. Next to him is the little god of convalescence, Telesphoros.

Hulton Getty Picture Collection, England.

place to another. Again, light is made to stream from the fingers
or hands, or miraculous supplies of food are provided. Inanimate
objects are made to act as if alive. Supernormal knowledge of
distant events or of men's thoughts is asserted. The power of
exorcizing and dispelling demons commonly occurs. Less rarely
the cure of disease and the removal of barrenness and even the
raising of the dead are found.[3]

Miracles of healing have been reported by many religions,
ancient and modern. But while the healing may in fact have happened, one must question whether the process should be assigned
to a supernatural agency or be attributed to powers that are resident in the human mind.

There is evidence that many of the spontaneous cures found in
medical practice are the result of suggestion. Once an idea has
been implanted and accepted, both the conscious and unconscious
mind exert an influence over the body, and thus is the physical
condition of the sufferer improved. The healing process, then,
reflects the power of the human mind rather than the intervention
of a sympathetic spirit.

And so it was expected that the advent of Christianity, like
other religions, brought with it numerous reports of miraculous
happenings. Christ, like Moses and Abraham before him, was
identified with miracles which both served to confirm his unique
position and suggested a resource that could be tapped by ordinary
men and women. And Christian saints followed suit, particularly
in the Middle Ages:

During the Middle Ages nothing seemed too incredible to be
related or believed. Every saint was expected to work miracles,
and miracles freely adorned the popular Lives of the saints. It
was said of Saint Vincent Ferrer that it was a miracle when he
performed no miracle. Any saint in whom a particular district,

Saint Brendan

Saint Brendan and fellow voyagers reportedly landed on the back of an obliging whale, having mistaken it for a small island.

Mary Evans Picture Library, London.

---

monastery, or church was interested was apt to have many miracles attributed to him. The people seemed incapable of being content with his spiritual victories; these had to take material form, to be symbolized as miracles. As in the earlier period, many miracles were alleged in support of particular doctrines or practices—the cult of the Virgin and saints, or relics, the Eucharist, the use of images. Protests were made from time to time by theologians, but in vain. The folk expected miracles, and miracles were freely provided for them. Many of the miracle stories are repeated in countless Lives of saints; one biographer plagiarized freely from another, and later Lives are often more full of miracles than the earlier Lives of the same saint. Biblical miracles were freely imitated; only in any given case they were multiplied a hundredfold. Other miracles belong to a floating tradition and repeat those already found in ethnic sources or in classical writings. Some are versions of folk-tale incidents. Frequently the quite ordinary or the particular gifts of a saint were exaggerated into miracles. Others can be traced to a misunderstanding of Christian artistic motifs—e.g., the stories of saints carrying their heads in their hands can be traced to pictures where they were thus represented to symbolize their death by decapitation—or to the visions or hallucinations of hysterical devotees, though these were supposed to belong to the highest state of ecstasy, in which reason played no part. All these miracles may be divided into four classes: (a) miracles wrought on nature, often of a most extravagant type—arresting the sun's course, hanging a cloak on a sunbeam; (b) miracles wrought by or upon inanimate objects—the numerous moving, talking, smiling images, already met with in paganism, or the opening of locked doors at the touch of a saint's finger; (c) miracles occurring to a saint—e.g., light streaming from his fingers, talking at birth, carrying fire, bilocation, levitation; and (d) miracles of healing, exorcism, and raising the dead.[4]

Many miracles were attributed to Francis Xavier (1506–1552) although, as a missionary in Indian and Japan, Xavier had never claimed miraculous powers, neither in conversation with his associates nor in the detailed accounts of his adventures which he carefully committed to writing. But, on his death, as sometimes happens in the case of religious figures, he was credited with curing the sick, casting out devils, and raising the dead—on quite a number of occasions.

For example, there was the matter of Xavier raising people from the dead. No mention of such a feat was made during Xavier's lifetime, neither in his own writing nor in the works of his contemporaries. But following Xavier's death there began to appear accounts of his former ability to raise people from the dead. It began with a single such account and grew as various Christian writers told the story of Xavier's sainted life; at the time of his canonization there were three such cases and in a biography written by Father Bouhours some one hundred thirty years after Xavier's death the count had risen to fourteen. Numerous other healing legends attached to Xavier, and all such stories were to convince the faithful that religion could cure their ills.

Finally, Xavier was canonized by the same pope who condemned Galileo, Urban VIII, who was particularly impressed by reports that a crucifix which Xavier had thrown on the waters to still a tempest was later returned to him by a crab; that a lamp filled only with holy water burned brightly before an image of Xavier; and that Xavier reportedly had possessed the gift of tongues, enabling him to spread the gospel across the lands of India and Japan. Yet Saint Xavier's own accounts often spoke of the problems he encountered with foreign languages and spoke of a delay in a certain trip when the interpreter he had hired failed to show up.

In our own culture a person may take one of three positions with respect to miracles: the theist believes in God and the possibility of divine intervention; the deist believes in God but not in divine intervention; and the atheist believes in neither. The theist will make the point that miracles are not improvisations or remedies for an imperfect world (implying a lack of foresight on the part of the Creator) but rather a manifestation of His presence and an act of salvation. We are told that: "Theology disapproves the suggestion by Sir Isaac Newton (1642–1727) that the Deity might occasionally intervene to make small adjustments to preserve the stability of the solar system—as if it were a car being serviced."[5]

Many professors of Christian theology no longer accept the traditional view of Christian miracles. Science and good scholarship have challenged the beliefs that had been held sacred for more than two thousand years. In particular, many miracles in the Old Testament are now thought to have been mythic in origin and may be found in the legends of other ancient religions. Other miracles may be traced to natural occurrences.

Man, Myth and Magic notes the probable source of many of the miracles reported in the Old Testament:

> The Red Sea can be forded or bypassed through the Reed Sea (now altered by the construction of the Suez Canal). Mount Sinai could have suggested a pillar of fire by night and cloud by day. The reference to the Israelites catching quails by hand, in the book of Numbers, is probable enough, for these birds can be caught in this way when exhausted; similarly manna, the food that sustained the people in the desert, can be collected from the tamarisk bush. . . . The Euphrates valley was flooded about 4000 B.C. and Noah's story is the legend of Utnapishtim, his Babylonian counterpart in the *Epic of Gilgamesh.* The mark of Cain was a clan-mark denoting blood-vengeance for slaying. The destruction of Sodom relates to volcanic activity and subsidence of the Dead Sea bed, while the story of Lot's wife being turned to salt was suggested by the salt slopes of the Dead Sea's banks. The birth story of Moses is that of King Sargon of Akkad (c 2300 b.c.). The story of Joseph and Potiphar's wife is the Egyptian Tale of the Two Brothers.[6]

The miracles attributed to Christ have also come under question, because their authenticity is based chiefly on the four Gospels. The *New Catholic Encyclopedia* notes that:

> Certitude as Historical. The factual evidence for the miracles of Christ is chiefly, though not exclusively, that provided by the four Gospels. While the Gospels were not meant to be strictly

scientific history, literally accurate in every detail, they are substantially historical. The demonstrable sincerity of the authors, their proximity to the events related, the concern of the primitive Christian community to safeguard the truth about its founder—these and other considerations provide an enduring guarantee of the reliability of the Gospel accounts.[7]

And yet in the earlier chapter on Holy Books it was seen that the authorship of the four Gospels is in some doubt today:

Yet today, there are few Biblical scholars—from liberal skeptics to conservative evangelicals—who believe that Matthew, Mark, Luke and John actually wrote the Gospels. Nowhere do the writers of the texts identify themselves by name or claim unambiguously to have known or traveled with Jesus. The majority of modern scholarly opinion holds that all four books were compiled from a variety of oral and written sources collected over a period of decades following Jesus' crucifixion, as the prologue to Luke suggests.[8]

The case for miracles is a difficult one to make, more so because those which are most central to Christian beliefs were reported two thousand years ago. The difficulty is shown, perhaps, in the Catholic position on non-Catholic miracles: "Whether or not there have been any certain miracles at all outside the Catholic Church is debatable. The vast majority of supposed cases on record are open to question from one standpoint or another—e.g., unreliable or insufficiently detailed testimony, the possibility of a purely natural explanation and in some instances strong indications of a diabolic origin."[9] Putting the possibility of a diabolic origin aside, science would raise the same objections to the reports of miracles by any religious denomination.

Overall, it would appear that the Christian belief in miracles is drawing to a close. After more than two thousand years, the claims of miraculous occurrences have been challenged by scientists and now are questioned by many Christian theologians as well. We are told that on the desk of Father Barraqué, the secretary-general of Lourdes, a sign reads: "Do It Yourself. God Can't Be Everywhere." Kenneth Woodward in his book *Making Saints* comments on the current attitude of the Roman Catholic Church: "Today, by contrast, the church is much more circumspect in its attitude toward the miraculous. As we will see, the modern saint-making process still requires miracles as signs of 'divine favor.' But it does not oblige Catholics to accept as a matter of 'supernatural' faith any purported miracle, including those worked at shrines like Lourdes or even those accepted in support of a saint's cause."[10] So today we may question what Webster defines as "an extraordinary event manifesting divine intervention in human affairs."

NOTES

1. James Hastings, ed., "Miracles," *The Encyclopaedia of Religion and Ethics* (New York: Charles Scribner and Sons, 1951), p. 677.

2. Joseph Campbell, *Myths to Live By* (New York: Bantam Books, 1973), p. 8.

3. Hastings, "Miracles," *Encyclopaedia of Religion and Ethics*, pp. 678, 685.

4. Ibid., p. 684.

5. Richard Cavendish, "Miracles," in *Man, Myth and Magic* (New York: Marshall Cavendish, 1970), p. 1744.

6. Ibid., p. 1745.

7. "Miracles," *New Catholic Encyclopedia* (New York: McGraw-Hill, 1967), p. 890.

8. "Who Wrote the Bible?" *U.S. News & World Report*, December 10, 1990, p. 63.

9. "Miracles," *New Catholic Encyclopedia*, p. 894.

10. Kenneth L. Woodward, *Making Saints* (New York: Simon and Schuster, 1990), p. 57.

13

Communion:
You Are What You Eat

cholars have found a widespread practice of consuming the gods sacramentally. Worshipers consume the human or animal who represents the god, or sometimes an image of the god made from bread. The origin of this religious custom is explained in *The Golden Bough*:

> The reasons for this partaking of the body of the god are, from the primitive standpoint, simple enough. The savage commonly believes that by eating the flesh of an animal or man he acquires not only the physical, but even the moral and intellectual qualities which were characteristic of that animal or man; so when the creature is deemed divine, our simple savage naturally expects to absorb a portion of its divinity, along with its material substance.[1]

The concept is sympathetic magic—the assumption that a person absorbs the characteristics of the animals he or she consumes. *The Golden Bough* mentions examples such as Caribs who abstained from eating pigs lest they should have the small eyes of a pig. In Northern India natives believe that eating the eyes of owls will help them to see in the dark. Brazilian Indians would eat no animal, bird, or fish that moved slowly, assuming they would become too slow to escape their enemies; West African men avoided tortoises for the same reason. Other African natives believe the flesh of hares could cause them to become fainthearted; they eat the flesh and drink the blood of lions and leopards to gain their strength. Some natives of northern Australia believe that eating the flesh of a kangaroo will make them jump higher and run faster. The Turks of Central Asia would feed their children the tongues of birds to help them learn to speak.

The flesh and blood of dead men are also eaten to benefit from their special qualities; many tribes around the world eat the heart of brave enemies killed in battle. A tribe in the mountains of Southeastern Africa has a menu of sorts for brave enemies: his liver is the seat of valor, his ears the center of intelligence, his testicles the source of strength—these are all made into a paste and eaten. In some savage cultures, sons would eat various parts of their departed fathers in order to preserve the strength and power of the loved one. Other primitive men would daub themselves with a dead man's blood to absorb his spirit. This is the basis for partaking of the body and blood of animals, humans, or gods. For example, the corn-god and the wine-god were represented by bread and wine which, when consumed, let the the worshiper share in the divine attributes of the gods. Apparently Cicero had reason to comment on this aspect of communion:

> When we call corn Ceres and wine Bacchus, we use a common figure of speech; but do you imagine that anybody is so insane as to believe that the things he feeds upon is a god?[2]

Early Communion

Many early peoples believed they would absorb, magically, the characteristics of the animals, or humans, or gods that they consumed.

Mary Evans Picture Library, London.

There are often laws to be observed before the act of communion with a deity. The stomach of the communicant, for example, must be prepared. The Creek and Seminole Indians took a purgative before swallowing the new corn representing the corn-god. The Masai of Eastern Africa swallow a very strong purgative and emetic to prepare for their gods. The object is to cleanse the stomach of common food before the deity is eaten. Similarly, Catholics fast before receiving their communion.

The Aztecs were eating bread sacramentally well before their conquest by the Spaniards. An image was made of dough and eaten by worshipers who believed they consumed the real bodies of the gods Huitzilopochtli or Vitzilipuztli. So even before the arrival of Christian missionaries the Aztec religion was acquainted with the idea of transubstantiation. That is, they believed their priests could turn bread dough into a god, and that those who ate the bread were consuming a god.

The Aryans of ancient India believed in the conversion of bread into the flesh of a human long before the spread of Christianity. In this case, the Brahmans believed that rice cakes could be offered in sacrifice and were real substitutes for human beings. When it was still rice meal it was thought to be hair, when water was added it became skin, when mixed into a paste it became flesh and when it was baked and became hard it was bone. Then it could be sprinkled with butter and it became marrow.

The ancient Cretans believed that Dionysus took the form of a bull, and had regular rites where the worshipers tore a live bull to bits with their teeth. Sir James Frazer comments: "We cannot doubt that in rending and devouring a live bull at his festival the worshipers of Dionysus believed themselves to be killing the god, eating his flesh, and drinking his blood."[3] Later his worshipers were to think that Dionysus had turned into a goat and again they devoured a raw goat as the body and blood of their god.

A number of scholars trace communion back to cannibalism,

where human victims were used to establish the bond between the gods and the worshipers. There are many examples where human sacrifices were accompanied by eating the victim in a ceremonial fashion. The Indian goddess Kali was frequently worshiped in this way.

Westermarck concludes that there is an obvious parallel between communion and the sacrificial form of cannibalism:

> The sacrificial form of cannibalism obviously springs from the idea that a victim offered to a supernatural being participates in his sanctity and from the wish of the worshiper to transfer to himself something of its benign virtue. So also the divine qualities of a man-god are supposed to be assimilated by the person who eats his flesh or drinks his blood. This was the idea of the early Christians concerning the Eucharist.[4]

Although earlier Christians regarded the Eucharist as the actual body and blood of a man-god, Christ, the Protestants began to raise questions in the sixteenth century when Martin Luther challenged the papacy on the reality of transubstantiation (that during mass the bread and wine literally became the body and blood of Jesus). Currently, most of the Catholic laity in America, if not the clergy, believe that the sacrament of Holy Communion is a symbolic reminder of Christ but not that bread and wine mysteriously turn into the actual body and blood of Christ. In fact, a *New York Times*/CBS poll taken in April 1994 notes that only one of three American Catholics believes in transubstantiation, so a core belief of Christianity has changed markedly over the centuries.

Communion, then, represents another religious belief that began among early peoples and gained stature over time. But its origin was in sympathetic magic and the curious assumption that a person absorbed the characteristics of the animals, humans, or gods that he or she consumed.

NOTES

1. Sir James G. Frazer, *The Golden Bough,* abridged ed. (New York: Macmillan Publishing Co., 1922), p. 573.

2. James Hastings, ed., "Communion," *The Encyclopaedia of Religion and Ethics* (New York: Charles Scribner and Sons, 1951), p. 770.

3. Frazer, *The Golden Bough,* p. 453.

4. Hastings, "Human Sacrifice," *The Encyclopaedia of Religion and Ethics,* p. 844.

14

Baptism:
The Wonders of Water

aptism is a religious rite that traces back to the earliest of times. Early humans saw the cleansing power of water and supposed that evil spirits could be washed from the body in the same manner as dirt. With time, the presumed powers of water became accepted and expanded to include washing away the enervating effects of sin and moral guilt. The use of water in baptismal rites has ranged from sprinkling to total submersion; its source has ranged from small vessels of holy water in temples to the sacred Ganges and the mighty oceans of the world.

Spittle has also been commonly used in baptismal rites. With the intention of establishing kinship with the newborn, indigenes spat upon the infant and rubbed their saliva into the body. Muhammad reportedly used spittle in baptizing one of his children, and folk-custom in medieval Europe held that spittle was particularly efficacious in keeping witches and fairies at bay and in counteracting the evil eye. The Roman Catholic Church once provided for the use of spittle in baptismal rites, but discontinued the practice in the 1960s.

As ancient means to purify and redeem an infant, water and spittle were joined by other substances such as blood, sand, and rice cakes. Blood was used in much the same way as spittle; it was assumed, based on sympathetic magic, that the qualities of a person could be transmitted by consuming the blood of that person or simply by coming into contact with the blood. One of the most dramatic baptismal rites in ancient times was the ceremony of the taurobolium in Rome, where people crouched below a raised platform to be drenched in the warm blood of a slain bull; the person was then *renatus in aeternum,* or "born again for eternity."

The reason for the baptism of infants began with the superstition that mothers and infants were particularly vulnerable to demons, and this belief may have been occasioned by the high infant mortality rates in ancient times. Some peoples were reluctant even to acknowledge a newborn infant for seven days, because so many died at birth; the departed infants were thought to have been "ghost babies" whom the spirits had reclaimed. Similarly, some European peasants were concerned that fairies would steal healthy babies and replace them with "changelings" who had puny little bodies. So the belief in devils, witches, and fairies led to a defense by baptism.

Baptism is also frequently the occasion for naming or renaming the child; the name was of great importance to early people because it was thought to be a part of one's personality. The combination of the name-giving ceremony with baptism is found in several African tribes, where immediately after birth a priest is sent for, whose job it is to decide which of the ancestors is residing in the body of the child; that determination having been made, the child is named accordingly, sprinkled with water, and presented to the tribe. Another tribe follows a similar procedure but allows both the priest and other tribesmen to talk with the ancestors and give

Jesus' Baptism

After Jesus was baptized, it is said that the Spirit of God descended on him in the form of a dove. An eighteenth-century manuscript.

The British Museum. Michael Holford Photographs, England.

one or more of their names to the infant. Afterward the child's forehead is touched with that of a cow, which then becomes the property of the child, who then becomes a member of the community. Among the Maoris, the priest repeated a number of ancestral names until the child sneezed, which was a signal from the ancestors that the correct name had been hit upon.

Thus the essential idea of baptism by water has persisted for thousands of years. It began with early people who believed that evil spirits could be rinsed from an infant's body, just as dirt is removed. Over the centuries, the superstition became formalized and gained acceptance as a well-established article of faith for many religions.

Within the overall Christian community, however, there is no agreement on infant baptism. Lutherans, Episcopalians, Methodists, Presbyterians, Catholics, among others, do baptize newborns. Baptists, Mormons, Seventh-Day Adventists, and Disciples of Christ believe that children should not be baptized until they are old enough to decide for themselves that they want to be baptized. Quakers do not practice water baptism at all.

The Roman Catholic Church places a special emphasis on infant baptism. The importance of baptism is clear from the Catholic belief that infants who die without baptism cannot enter heaven; instead they are destined to stay forever in limbo. Saint Augustine went further and asserted that unbaptized children would suffer the fires of hell for all eternity. The Catholic doctrine of Original Sin asserts that all newborn infants inherit the sins of Adam, and without the redemption of baptism are doomed never to see heaven.

The Aztecs believed in being born again through baptism and, somewhat like Catholics, believed that sin was acquired before the creation of the world, or before the person was born. In either case, the words and the baptism by water removed the inherited sin and freed the Aztec child from evil spirits. Again, an ancient Aztec prayer is very similar to a modern Christian baptismal prayer:

A Christian Prayer

Almighty and everlasting God, who of thy great mercy didst save Noah and his family in the ark from perishing by water; and also didst safely lead the children of Israel thy people through the Red Sea, figuring thereby the Holy baptism; and by the Baptism of thy well-beloved Son Jesus Christ, in the river Jordan, didst sanctify Water to the mystical washing away of sin; We beseech thee, for thine infinite mercies, that thou wilt mercifully look upon this Child; wash him and sanctify him with the Holy Ghost. . . .

(The Book of Common Prayer)

An Aztec Prayer
(From the Aztec ceremony of bathing the newborn)

Merciful Lady Chalchiuhtlicue, thy servant here present is come into the world . . . wash him and deliver him from impurities. . . . Cleanse him of the contamination he hath received from his parents: let the water take away the soil and the stain, and let him be freed from all taint. May it please thee, O Goddess, that his heart and his life be purified, that he may dwell in this world in peace and wisdom. May this water take away all ills . . . wash from him the evils which he beareth from before the beginning of the world.

(Bernardino de Sahagun,
Historia de las Cosas de la Nueva España)

So the purpose of baptism is ancient and universal: to protect the child from evil spirits and to cleanse the child from impurities, taboos, or inherited sin. The use of water, from immersion to sprinkling, the dedication of the child to a god, the role of the priest or medicine man, and the social and public aspects of the ceremonies are similar around the world. It may be concluded from both the antiquity and universality of the baptismal rites that Jewish, Christian, Muslim, and other living religions have borrowed from the primitive and pagan cultures.

15

Circumcision:
A Mark on Mankind

The origin of circumcision and related mutilations of the sexual organs was both ancient and widespread. The practice is often attributed to a preoccupation with sexual matters among early peoples and was often associated with rites of puberty. Some eminent psychologists have speculated that circumcisions and other painful initiations into adulthood are expressions of adult dominance over children.

It does appear that circumcision originated in the most rudimentary levels of civilization; when these same cultures advanced to a more civilized and less superstitious stage, circumcision was carried forward but then with a religious motive to justify the tradition.

In Africa, as young boys and girls approach puberty they are given special training to equip them for their adult roles, including training in sexual behavior. The puberty rites for boys often include circumcision, which the youngster is expected to endure without crying out. Female circumcision is also practiced by a number of tribes although this practice is on the wane; the female circumcision may be a clitoridectomy or mutilation of the labia.

An apparent lack of sophistication by tribes practicing circumcision is best seen, perhaps, by the Australian tribe which carefully preserved the male foreskins in the fat of a wild dog and of a carpet snake for later use in ceremonies to produce rain. Certain native queens were known to have necklaces made from the foreskins of the youth.

Circumcision is one of a number of mutilations used by indigenous peoples around the world:

Circumcision	The male prepuce is abscised or the female external genitalia excised.
Filing or removing teeth	Teeth are filed to sharp points or knocked out above or below.
Perforating lips or ears	Lips or ears are perforated for the insertion of an ornament.
Scarification and tattoos	Faces and bodies are scarred; punctures filled with blood or ash to render them indelible.
Dilatatio vaginal or artificial defloration	The vagina is enlarged by cutting or the girls are artificially deflowered.
Infibulation	Sewing together of parts of the vulva.

Other than mutilations, initiation and puberty rites often included tests of endurance where the young men were forced to wear collars of thorns, given beatings, deprived of sleep, exposed to bites of poisonous ants, or required to kill someone. Young girls

Early Circumcision

Relief from a tomb at Saqqara that shows a young Egyptian being circumcised with a flint knife. The Sixth Dynasty, Old Kingdom.

The Oriental Institute of the University of Chicago. The University of California Press, Berkeley; Occasional Papers Number 11 Archeology.

were sometimes forced to live in isolation for a year, or be contained in cages. Initiates were often blackened with charcoal or daubed with clay or painted in distinctive patterns, and the final ceremonies saw them ceremonially washed and dressed with fitting ornaments. The final ceremony frequently included a religious service, a feast and dancing, and often sexual intercourse. As circumcision serves no particular purpose, some fashion authorities assume that it falls into the category of customizing the human body for purposes of distinctiveness and fashion:

> But what the human race has come up with in the way of clothing to proclaim status pales before the ingenuity exercised, at one time or another, to customize the human body. The morbid pastime of cutting, painting, constricting, and otherwise improving on basic anatomy is probably rooted in protective magic. The still-common practice of circumcision, for all the medical tootle about health and hygiene, would seem to confirm this. In Egypt, parts of Africa and the Americas, heads of infants were bound to produce an elegantly sloping cranium. Mayan infants had a bead tied to a strand of hair hanging down over their nose to ensure a fashionable cross-eyed glare when they grew up. Constrictive leg bandages were used in the Caribbean and arm rings in Melanesia, forcing the muscles to bulge mightily on either side. Tattooing has been widely practiced in all parts of the globe; a full tattoo suit can still be seen, though rarely, in downtown Tokyo. Body scarification, though less common, can still be found in Africa, particularly among Dahomean ladies of rank who allow themselves to be carved like a Christmas goose for purely cosmetic purposes. Men and women have worn ear spools so enormous that an arm could be inserted through the distorted lobe; nose ornaments that pierced and distorted the septum were once popular; front teeth have been filed to elegant points or knocked out altogether to accommodate ornate lip jewels.

As might be expected, women suffered the worst. In provincial African courts at the turn of the century, young girls were force-fattened to hopeless obesity. The wives of the king of Karagwe could not stand up; the explorer John Speke commented of one, "her features were lovely but her body was as round as a ball." In old China, the feet of high-born women were cruelly bound and compressed to form the prestigious Golden Lilies. Her bride price depended directly upon the size of her feet; her tiny shoes were exhibited to the prospective in-laws during the marriage negotiations. From the age of three or four until death, there was no respite from constant, tormenting agony.[1]

The Jews had, of course, practiced circumcision of the male from early in the worship of the patriarchs and regarded circumcision as a mandate from God to the Jews, beginning with God's commandment to Abraham (Gen. 17:10, 11). However, it is not clear whether the Israelites borrowed the practice of circumcision from the ancient Egyptians, or whether both learned the custom from still more ancient societies. Scholars do believe that the practice was quite ancient and widespread and probably predated Abraham.

Although Jews were well known for the practice of circumcision, in earlier days it did not go without comment. The Greeks believed in the beauty of the unmarred human body and Jewish circumcision was the object of humor. Certainly circumcision stands out as one of the more curious of the religious rites, either from the standpoint of its relevance to moral values or its significance to a Supreme Being. Nevertheless, for thousands of years, circumcision has left its mark on mankind.

NOTE

1. Rachel H. Kemper, *Costume* (New York: Newsweek Books, 1977), p. 14.

16

Exorcism:
A Defense against Demons

An inability to explain natural phenomena led early humans to assume the existence of controlling spirits. Water, wind, trees—virtually every object in nature—was thought to be activated by unseen spirits. It followed that animals and humans were also thought to be possessed by spirits. The evidence of human possession was any action that seemed uncharacteristic of that person and, as a result, mental and physical disturbances were often taken to be the work of demons.

Exorcism was the means of removing the offending spirits from their habitat. People believed that priests or medicine men had the ability to transfer spirits from one place to another by means of certain rituals and prayers. The priest was usually able to speak personally with the demon, elicit certain information, and then establish his authority to expel the demon by virtue of his association with a more powerful spirit.

Buddhist priests trained hard for their role as exorcists and brought to bear fasting, chanting, and the use of magic castanets which were believed to have a dramatic effect on spirits. Successful exorcisms have been reported wherein, for example, a demon who spoke in the voices of a fox, cat, snake, and woman was first exorcised and later begged forgiveness and began to recite holy scripture.

Ancient China used similar means to exorcise spirits, with Taoist priests and some Buddhist priests performing before altars to the beat of drums and smell of incense, dancing and spitting water in controlled streams at the four cardinal directions. When Confucianism became the state religion of China, the educated tended to look at exorcism as an entertainment rather than a serious religious rite, but the population as a whole retained its belief in exorcism.

Indian holy books described how demons could be driven from the body and returned to their source or transferred to a tree, animal, or another human being. Indians also tempted the demon to depart a person's body with sweetmeats and sacrifices but, this failing, were prepared to beat the sufferer or apply red pepper to his or her nostrils to hasten the departure of the spirits.

Overall, a number of imaginative approaches were used to drive away the demons. As the Roman Catholic priest once blew on the newborn infant to chase away the devil, the Siberian shamans blew on corpses to rid them of demons, while their assistants maintained a rhythmic drum beat and cried, "Begone."

A number of African tribes report cases of possession where the spirits demand, through the lips of an unfortunate woman, clothing, jewelry, and perfume. When this possession is identified by the exorcist, the husband of the stricken woman pays large sums of money to bring relief. Similar possessions have been reported in Japan and have been diagnosed by some as an unconscious attempt by the women to protest against their neglect in a male-dominated society.

Some tribes in West Africa expel spirits by their transference to a scapegoat, reminiscent of the Hebrew practice. In one such case, a mother who lost her twins was dusted on the brow, breasts, knees, and feet with a fowl and then told to hold a goat by the horns and touch foreheads three times. The fowl and goat were then set loose and presumably took the evil spirits with them into the jungle.

The Islamic world recognizes both licit and illicit exorcists, depending on whether the spirits are controlled by supplicating God and his powers or by performing acts that are displeasing to God. The name of the sufferer is also influential, as it is related to the signs of the Zodiac, the seven planets, and the four elements.

The Jews of the Old Testament made little reference to possession and exorcism. Sarah, for example, although guarded by a demon was not possessed by one. But by the time of Christ the practice of exorcism was well established among the Jews.

CHRISTIAN EXORCISM

The Christian religion gave considerable impetus to the practice of exorcism. Apparently exorcism began and spread throughout Christianity based on the New Testament accounts, for example: "In my name shall they cast out devils" (Mark 16:17; also Luke 9:1; 10:17). And the reputation of the early Christian exorcists helped to spread the Christian faith.

As it happens, religions around the world tend to identify the invading spirits as local spirits subject to the local gods, and so it was with Christianity:

In Catholic demonology, possession by any evil spirit became limited to possession by a Christian devil. As a Christian devil, he admitted the superior power of the Christian God and therefore obeyed the commands of a Christian priest acting through exorcism on behalf of God and the Church. Yet the Christian rites of exorcism are not fundamentally different from similar ceremonies in other religions against possession by the demons of those religions.[1]

The early Christian ceremonies to exorcise demons were relatively simple and involved a litany, prayers, and the laying on of hands. Origen in the third century C.E. credited the letters of the word *Jesus* with expelling evil spirits from countless people whose souls were possessed, simply by virtue of the power of the name. One evidence of the power of the early exorcists is noted in Jerome's *Life of Saint Hilary*, who lived about 390 C.E.:

Brute animals were also daily brought to him in a state of madness, and among them a Bactrian camel of enormous size, amid the shouts of thirty men or more who held him tight with stout ropes. He had already injured many. His eyes were bloodshot, his mouth filled with foam, his rolling tongue swollen, and above every other source of terror was his loud and hideous roar. Well, the old man ordered him to be let go. At once those who had brought him as well as the attendants of the saint fled away without exception. The saint went by himself to meet him, and addressing him in Syriac said, "You do not alarm me, devil, huge though your present body is. Whether in a fox or a camel you are just the same." Meanwhile he stood with outstretched hand. The brute, raging and looking as if he would devour Hilary, came up to him, but immediately fell down, laid its head on the ground, and to the amazement of all present showed suddenly no less tameness than it had exhibited ferocity before. But the old man declared to them how the devil, for men's account, seizes even beasts of burden; that he is inflamed by such intense hatred for men that he desires to destroy not only them but what belongs to them.[2]

Exorcising Spirits

Detail from Botticelli's painting of Saint Zenobius exorcising evil spirits, which issue from the victims' mouths in the form of black imps.

The National Gallery Picture Library, National Gallery Publications Limited.

Christian exorcism began with a decision on whether the possessing spirit was good or evil. The *Enchiridium,* a manual of exorcism compiled by a Vincentius von Berg, noted a number of tests that may be used to establish malignancy. The spirit was evil if it:

- Said anything against the Catholic faith.
- Fled at the sign of the cross, holy water, the name of Jesus, etc.
- Refused to discuss the possession with a priest.
- Appeared with a loathsome or dejected appearance, or departed leaving a stench, noise, frightfulness, or injury.

Still other criteria are cited by the *Encyclopedia of Witchcraft and Demonology,* but all of the same drift. The *Enchiridium* also told how to determine whether the devil had entered the body through his own volition or whether the devil had been induced to take possession by witchcraft. If witches were involved, the possessed person generally complained of bodily aches and pains, weakness, melancholy, or other evidence of mental or physical malaise. The exorcist was also responsible for establishing a dialogue of sorts with the demons, first, by insisting on solid evidence of possession:

> I, N., minister of Christ and the church, in the name of Jesus Christ, command you, unclean spirit, if you lie hid in the body of this man created by God, or if you vex him in any way, that immediately you give me some manifest sign of the certainty of your presence in possessing this man . . . which heretofore in my absence you have been able to accomplish in your accustomed manner. (*Enchiridium*)

When possession was clearly established, the priest was required to ask the devil his name, how many devils were involved, why the possession had taken place, the exact time that the devil had entered the body, and whether it was the devil's intent to stay a specified time or forever. For example, in a difficult exorcism in 1618, a corps of Dominicans, Jesuits, and Capuchins were administering to a French noblewoman with these results:

> The spirit . . . commenced to speak with great difficulty through the mouth of the patient, and we commenced to interrogate it in this manner:
>
> What was his name; where he came from, and what his region. He replied to this command given him through the power of God that his name was Mahonin, of the third hierarchy, and the second order of archangels, and that his living, before he entered the body of the possessed, was in the water.
>
> Conjured to say what saint in heaven was his adversary, he replied it was Saint Mark the Evangelist. . . .
>
> Interrogated of what place he was native, said Beziers, town in Languedoc, on the Spanish frontier. . . .
>
> Questioned on what day he had entered the body, said it was the third Tuesday of last Easter in the month of March, when the said possessed lady was in the town of Agen. . . .
>
> Questioned how long was the bewitchment, said for two years. . . .
>
> "Commanded to give a sign when he would depart, replied he would give one by throwing a stone from the tower into the water of the moat. (*Les Conjurations faites a un demon possedant le corps d'une grande dame* [Paris: J. Mesmier, 1619])[3]

There exists a Christian *Thesaurus Exorcismorum* which describes the proper approach to any possession by evil spirits. Included are exorcisms to protect a house from demons, to stabilize a marriage where the devil is at work, to cure sicknesses of all description, to ward off insects such as locusts, and to avoid a cow going dry. There are also the more exotic complaints of some who require spiritual remedies against succubus and incubus demons.

In some cases strong language was used to revile the demon as a "lean sow, mangy beast, dingy collier, swollen toad or lousy swineherd." Fumigation was used on occasion, as was flagellation; some religious authorities in the 1600s recommended moderate flagellation not so much to expel the demons as to show contempt for them.

Exorcism has been practiced by Christians since the church was founded and was undiminished over the many centuries. During the European witch persecutions from 1484 to 1648 exorcism reached a high point. In another example:

> Apart from the notorious case of the devils of Loudun, there were many instances of exorcism upon doubtful subjects. In 1618 a young widow, Elisabeth de Renfaing, while on pilgrimage to a shrine in Lorraine accused another pilgrim, one Dr. Poirot, of trying to bewitch her. He fled in alarm, was caught at the frontier and, flight being taken as admission of guilt, was put to death. The lady was exorcized by two Sorbonne theologians. She spoke in English to a lay brother from the English Benedictines at Dieuleward with whom she was confronted, floated up to the roof of the chapel and performed other prodigies. Later she settled down to found a convent at Nancy (which is still there) and to care for the reformed prostitutes of the town.[4]

Most Protestant churches have rejected the idea of demonic possession and exorcism, although the Roman Catholic Church maintains its belief in the concepts. In 1947 Francis Cardinal Spellman wrote the introduction to the *Rituale Romanum*, which was a verbatim reproduction of the rite of exorcism printed in 1619. The entire rite is shown in the *Encyclopedia of Witchcraft and Demonology*. A long and impressive ceremony, it begins by imploring God's grace against the "wicked dragon" and a demand to the possessing spirit to "tell me thy name, the day, and the hour of thy going out, by some sign."

The *New Catholic Encyclopedia* summarizes the Church's position today:

> In the performance of an exorcism it is always the Church that prays through the instrumentality of the exorcist, so that the efficacy of the rite is analogous to that of the sacramentals. At the same time, it is obvious from the Gospels themselves that the exorcist's faith and integrity play a determining role in the outcome of the exorcism (Mt 17.14–20; Mk 9.13–28; Lk 9. 37–43). For this reason the Church exercises the greatest caution in authorizing clerics who have received the power of exorcism through Holy Orders to put it to use. This is not true, of course, of exorcisms employed during the rite of Baptism, but of those uses of the power that an apparently authentic instance of possession has required. Of those cases of possession against which exorcism proves to be ineffective, one can only say that an error of judgment has been made as to the true nature of the phenomenon or that for reasons of His own God has withheld the rite's efficacy. Recourse to this latter explanation should be infrequent, to say the least, since the question of the Church's ability to carry on the essential work of its founder and master is at issue.
>
> Exorcisms are rarely performed today, not because the Church has lost its belief in the power and activity of Satan but because it recognizes that true cases of possession are rare. What often appeared to be possession in earlier ages is now recognized as a pathological state attributable to one or more nervous disorders, and for these the proper remedies are neurology, psychiatry, or depth psychology.[5]

A significant change has taken place in the opinions of Christians who, in past centuries, were totally committed to the idea of demonic possession and exorcism. As noted before, Christianity owed much of its early popularity to a reputation for effective exorcism. In current times, Christian theologians are divided on the certain efficacy of exorcism. For example, in 1993 Ted Koppel hosted a television show on exorcism in which the chair of theology at Notre Dame University called the Church's historical views on demonic possession "an embarrassment."

The issue is larger than a single religious rite, of course, because it bears on a fundamental aspect of religion: a raison d'etre of religion is the existence of evil spirits and the ability of the Church to control them. If offending spirits no longer have to be taken into account, then religion stands to lose much of its former value for men and women.

NOTES

1. Russell Hope Robbins, "Exorcism," *The Encyclopedia of Witchcraft and Demonology* (New York: Crown Publishers, 1959), p. 180.

2. Ibid.

3. Ibid., p. 185.

4. Richard Cavendish, "Exorcism," *Man, Myth and Magic* (New York: Marshall Cavendish Corporation, 1983), p. 873.

5. "Exorcism," *New Catholic Encyclopedia* (New York: McGraw-Hill, 1967), p. 749.

17

Asceticism:
Or No Pain, No Gain

Many of today's religions were built on an idea of suffering and self-inflicted pain. Indeed, the great heroes of the faith were often martyrs and ascetics who, to improve and display their holiness, punished their minds and bodies.

Not every religion is committed to the idea of asceticism. Some have found an apparent contradiction in despising a body, or a world, created by their god. But asceticism is widespread and has formed the basis for much religious belief.

PERSIAN

The prophet Zoroaster took a strong stand against asceticism. He taught that marriage and family were superior to the unmarried state, that owning a home was better than being homeless, that fasting was a sin. And Zoroastrianism expressly forbade mortification of the flesh. Penance, if needed, included: "He must make ditches for irrigation, and make a gift to good men of cultivated ground and a beautiful bedstead. . . . He must give a young virgin as wife to a good man. . . . He must make a gift of small cattle. . . . He has to bring up seven puppies. . . ."[1]

JEWISH

Even in the early Jewish beliefs, no asceticism was required to achieve the highest state of holiness. The world was not to be renounced, and no mortification of the flesh was required; actually, as the body was deemed sacred, mutilation was forbidden. Fasting was an accompaniment of prayer and confession, but it was not used as a self-inflicted punishment. Marriage and a family were encouraged, not continence. Overall, the Jewish philosophy was not to separate oneself from the world but rather to enjoy the blessings of life.

MUSLIM

Muhammad did not advocate asceticism. The Prophet enjoyed life to the full and gave his followers license within certain limits. Restrictions were placed on intoxicating drinks and requirements did call for five daily prayers and a pilgrimage to Mecca. But the social and enthusiastic spirit of Islam were in contrast to the withdrawn and penitent attitude of Christianity.

There were a few early examples of asceticism, such as undertaking the pilgrimage to Mecca without shoes, or of pilgrims letting themselves be led around the sacred Kaba like a camel by means of a ring inserted in the nose. But these were not a formal part of the religion.

In time, however, an ascetic movement began and spread among many Muslims. Sufism was orthodox in the beginning but became mystical and sought direct experience with Allah through ascetic practices. The early Sufis were attracted to asceticism mainly because of the terror inspired by the Quran—God's revelation to Muhammad—and its descriptions of the Day of Judgment and the tortures of Hell. This led to a morbid consciousness of sin.

The asceticism of the Sufis followed a fairly typical course with the wearing of uncomfortable woolen garments, fasting, renunciation of the world, and vows of poverty. One leader would knock his head against the wall until it bled, another would flagellate himself when his concentration failed. In the twelfth century, the Sufis began to organize into monastical orders and a member was known as a fakir or a dervish. In some cases, asceticism went to odd extremes with Sufis swallowing live coals or snakes. The Turkish dervishes became well known for seeking union with God by whirling in one spot for hours.

BUDDHIST

The Buddhists have believed in a Middle Path, neither extreme indulgence in the sensual pleasures of life nor extreme deprivation or self-mortification. Both extremes were taught by Buddha to be ignoble, based on his own personal experiences.

Buddhism does have ascetics, but not in the sense of their employing hard penance, isolation, or tedium. The Buddhist ascetic is more concerned with an appropriate discipline of thought and action that will lead to an improvement in the individual. This attitude is similar to that of the Greeks, whose definition of asceticism was more an ability to reject a lesser good in favor of a greater good. Training, mental discipline, and good health are the avenues.

HINDU

The underlying personality of the Indian people has been described as high-strung, passionate, and pleasure seeking. The supposition is that where emotion and desire hold sway so emphati-
cally, one should expect to find a similar excess in attempts to
temper exuberance. It is certainly true that India has led all efforts
to suppress the gratification of the senses. Pain has become an art
and asceticism rules most daily acts in life. The ascetic is held in
high esteem.

The ascetic life is prompted by the desire to escape the never-
ending cycle of reincarnation, or at least to improve on one's position in the various stages. The austerities are clearly described. An
ascetic begins by giving away all earthly belongings save a simple
garment, a bowl for begging food, and usually a staff. Even when
eating, religious law provides for eight mouthfuls for a true ascetic,
sixteen mouthfuls for a hermit in the woods, and an unlimited
quantity of food for students.

The body of the ascetic will be rubbed with ashes, not unlike
the Christian tradition, as a defense against demons. A rosary is
usually carried to help with the recitation of prayers; beads may
take the form of human teeth or seeds of the sacred lotus.

Self-mortification has taken many turns. Ancient Hindu
ascetics might stand on one leg all day, immovable in the heat of
the sun. One ascetic is said to have lain naked on a couch for
thirty-five years. A common form of self-torture is to raise one or
both arms above the head until they atrophy and cannot be low-
ered. The hand is sometimes held closed until the fingernails grow
through the palm. Some of the greatest hardships are suffering
from want of food and cold. Skewers may be stuck into the flesh,
or the ascetic may eat live coals. Some volunteer to be buried alive
or hung with their heads down. There is almost no end to the imaginative forms of self-mortification.

There are believed to be few Aghorins now left in India, but from an early date these ascetics were committed to eating the flesh of corpses whose bodies were taken from the graveyard or from the river.

Through renunciation of the world and a program of self-torture, the ascetic hopes to escape the endless cycle of reincarnations and to develop supernatural powers. In fact, marvelous feats of physical endurance and mental discipline have been achieved.

Perhaps five million ascetics lived in India at the beginning of the twentieth century. The number may have increased over time because originally the right of asceticism belonged only to the priest-class, or Brahmins; now men of every class may become ascetic.

ANCIENT GREEK AND ROMAN

There were very early traces of asceticism in Greek culture, as far back as the seventh century B.C.E. But the real beginning was with the Dionysian cult, whose members went into ecstatic trances. Dionysus was the Greek god of wine and liberation, and was frequently associated with fertility symbols such as satyrs, goats, and bulls.

The Dionysian cult proposed the idea that the body was in opposition to the soul. The idea of an independent soul came from early humans, probably based on their dreams about the deceased where the dead appeared "in spirit." The Dionysian cult suggested that the soul was not only independent of the body but could reach new heights of ecstasy if freed from bodily restraints. The body therefore became the enemy of the soul, and the soul could be purified by assaulting and denying the body. Such a belief is the beginning and the very essence of asceticism.

Orphic and Pythagorean cults followed the Dionysian cult until Empedocles added further refinements to the concept of soul and body. Empedocles taught that the soul fell from its divine condition into the body of humans, and the soul must do penance by working its way through the bodies of humans, animals, and plants. Asceticism was thought to be an effective way of delivering the soul from its bodily environs and beginning its pilgrimage. It may be noted that the migration of the soul into trees and plants excluded beans—an exclusion held by the Orphics and Pythagoreans, as well.

The Greek philosophers Plato and Socrates took over the idea of the soul and gave further credence to the idea that the body restrains the soul. Other schools, such as the Cynics and Stoics, also gave thought to the ideas of world-renunciation and the possibilities of ascetic behavior.

The Cynics showed their ascetical tendencies by a simple life, eating mostly dried figs and peeled barley, and often sleeping in the open air. History notes, however, that a distinctly Hellenic feature of the discipline was an open attitude toward sex. The Cynics regarded sex as a natural impulse or appetite, and Diogenes satisfied his hunger through masturbation or intercourse, sometimes in the presence of onlookers and apparently without embarrassment.

The early Greek thought seemed to conclude with the original concept of dualism: the soul was the spirit of good, the body was evil. Asceticism was the means for the soul to prevail over the body.

Roman thought on the subject reflected a general acceptance of the Greek ideas, with a number of variations. And, from what began with the Dionysian cult in about 300 B.C.E., the stage was set for Christian asceticism.

CHRISTIAN

Early Christianity departed from the Judaic tradition and adopted asceticism as a means of becoming holier. Apparently the early

Anthony's Demons

Schongauer's *Temptation of St. Anthony* illustrates the struggles of the saint against the demons who reportedly sought to overcome him.

The British Museum, London.

Christians found their models and motives for asceticism in pagan Hellenism.

The rise of religious asceticism in the second century was associated with the oriental mystery religions, especially those of Attis-Cybele and Isis. Priests of Attis regularly castrated themselves in the service of their god. They also engaged in such rites as the "Day of Blood" when the high priest drew blood from his arm, following which the inferior clergy gashed themselves in a frenzy of excitement and movement to music of a wild barbarian strain.

The ideal of Christian asceticism was martyrdom or, short of that, an imitation of Christ's suffering that would somehow result in a mystical union with God. The early Christian Church had a contempt for the material world, a negative attitude toward marriage, and taught that certain sins could never be forgiven.

Origen was a prominent Christian teacher, writer, and theologian in the second century. As a youth, he emasculated himself in an excess of ascetic zeal, and he continued throughout his life to encourage mortification of the flesh and renunciation of the world. He took severe positions on fasting and taught lifelong virginity. Origen found three kinds of God-pleasing sacrifice of special worth: a martyr death, voluntary celibacy, and abstinence from sexual intercourse by married persons.

In the latter part of the third century, Saint Anthony of Egypt set an example of seclusion, self-denial, and prayer by living in the desert. This began a movement to coenobitism (a hermit's life) and eventually to monasticism. Poverty, chastity, and obedience were and are the characteristics of the monastic life. In the fourth century monasteries for men were joined by nunneries for women. Beginning in the eleventh century many monastic orders intensified their asceticism by adding the penalty of flagellation, with many unseemly refinements in its use. Self-flagellation began at that time, along with other forms of self-torture. Ascetic practices multiplied from 1100 to 1500, with both sexes resorting to practices such as inclusio, or allowing oneself to be shut up in narrow cells or caves with almost no room for movement. During this same period, the flagellants would display their asceticism in great processions over the lands.

The idea and excesses of asceticism became almost epidemic at that point. The *Encyclopaedia of Religion and Ethics* describes this asceticism and kindred phenomena as betraying "a religious degeneration, hand in hand with which went numerous symptoms of moral decay, particularly in the discipline of most of the religious orders, old and new alike."

There were many curious examples of asceticism during this period:

> Some of the austerities recorded of Irish saints are as follows: St. Finnchua is said to have spent seven years suspended by iron shackles under his armpits, "so that he might get a place in heaven," in lieu of one which he had given away. Both he and St. Ite are said to have caused their bodies to be eaten into by chafers or stag-beetles. St. Findian is said to have worn a girdle of iron that cut to the bone. Of St. Ciaran we are told that he mixed his bread with sand, and of him and St. Columba that they slept on the ground with a stone for a bolster. Of St. Mochua it is said that he lived as an inclusus in a prison of stone, and that he had only a little aperture left for letting food down to him. Of the Welsh saint Brynach we are told that he lessened his need for the luxury of clothing by dipping his body daily in the coldest water, and St. Cadoc is also said to have been wasted with fastings. Further, of the Irish saint Kevin it is said that he remained for seven years in a standing posture without sleep, with his arm held up in the same position, and that a blackbird laid and hatched her eggs in his palm.[2]

So Christian asceticism has taken many forms. Fasting had its origin among early peoples who thought that food contained evil spirits and would contaminate their body prior to worshiping their god. Sexual continence was prescribed because sex was linked with life and the religious were taught to despise an earthly existence. Isolation was another renunciation of the world, undertaken to avoid sin and distraction and to punish the body's senses. Self-torture and pain were a way to rid the body of demons while accepting a deserved punishment for sin.

Asceticism in its more extreme forms is a perversion of a natural inclination to avoid pain. Today it is recognized for its psychopathological elements in which pain is a source of sexual pleasure. But in the Middle Ages, the ascetic activities of religious saints were not identified with the masochistic impulses now seen in mental hospitals; instead, asceticism was regarded as evidence of unusual piety and close communion with God.

Today's anthropologists do not believe in the concept of asceticism. It appears that most Protestant theologians as well are not persuaded of its value. There is still some support for asceticism among Catholic theologians, although not to the degree of old.

The tradition and sentiment in the Catholic Church that speaks for asceticism, if in a modified form, is explained in the *New Catholic Encyclopedia*:

> Asceticism is not merely an exercise of self-mastery or a struggle against the passions; neither is it a mere subjection of the body to the spirit. Granted, the struggle is against human weakness and instability; yet when the Scriptures speak of the war against "the flesh" they do not mean against bodiliness, but against the existential condition of fallen man, proud and self-centered. Implied in this are all the forces of perdition: original sin, the burden of personal sins for which one is still insufficiently repentant and for which he has not yet sufficiently atoned, the social milieu formed by one's sins and the sins of others that tends to draw one downward, and the fallen angels,

who exercise their powers in the world. For our wrestling is not against flesh and blood, but against the Principalities and Powers, against the world-rulers of this darkness, against the spiritual forces of wickedness on high.[3]

NOTES

1. James Hastings, ed., "Asceticism," *The Encyclopaedia of Religion and Ethics* (New York: Charles Scribner and Sons, 1951), p. 106.

2. Ibid., p. 72.

3. "Asceticism," *New Catholic Encyclopedia* (New York: McGraw-Hill, 1967), p. 942.

18

The Body:
Hands, Heads, and Phalli

HANDS

*T*he hand has always had a special place in magical and religious rites. In ancient Egypt, the symbol for the powerful sun-god was the sun's rays ending in the shape of hands. The Indian god Savitar was described as having a hand that covered boundless areas of heaven. In many religions, the hand of a god, frequently emerging from the clouds, symbolized the power of a supreme being. Numerous gods had extra hands or fingers as evidence of their great power.

The ancient Hindus associated each part of the hand—thumb, little finger, fingertips—with gods; the modern Hindu believes that various parts of the hand are sacred to Vishnu. The ancient Arabs caressed the household god with their hands when entering or leaving. Likewise, Jews touched the mezuzah, or doorpost, with the forefinger when entering or leaving the house. The Roman

Catholic priests continue to have their hands consecrated and sanctified; their hands are used for benediction, confirmation, ordination, baptism, anointing, exorcism, and absolution.

The custom of healing with hands goes back to prehistoric times. Even in ancient Babylon, the evil spirits were exorcised by the priest laying hands on the head of the sick man. The ancient Egyptians conferred the blessings of the gods by laying on hands. The Arabs also conveyed blessings with hands and the Jews transferred sin from a person to a scapegoat with hands. Following the primitive tradition, Christ and the Apostles also used hands in healing and in conferring special powers (e.g., Matthew 9:18, Mark 16:18, 1 Timothy 4:14). And the custom of laying on hands continues even today.

In many religions the hand, in various gestures, may cast a spell or protect against it. To this day it is impolite to point one's forefinger at someone because this finger was thought to have a magical power, as when the power would stream from the magician's finger to his victim. Bloody hands were often found on doors of buildings or temples to protect against witchcraft or prevent the entrance of evil spirits; they were painted or were the impressions of a hand actually dipped in blood. Such bloody hands have been used by Babylonians, Phoenicians, Egyptians, Jews, Muslims, Japanese, and Italians.

According to the principles of contagious magic, a severed part of the body can still exert an influence on the whole. Thus Hebrews, Egyptians, Teutons, and some American Indians cut off the hands or fingers of slain enemies as trophies and as ways to further torment their former adversaries. Similarly, hands or fingers would be cut off living persons as a punishment and the mutilation was thought to adversely affect the person's ghost in the afterlife. In West Africa, natives often kept human hands in their fetish-bags as relics. Pliny was said to have referred to the power of a dead hand as a healing charm. Muhammadan women in Egypt wore the dried finger of a Jew or Christian as a cure for the ague.

Hands are of particular importance in taking an oath. The hands are placed on some sacred object, on the assumption that the sacred object will somehow harm the person if the vow is broken. Samoans, for example, place their hands on a sacred stone. Modern Christians, Muslims, and Jews place their hands on a sacred book. The ancient Hebrews placed their hands on their generative organs when taking an oath.

Both magic and religion usually call for the purification of hands before and sometimes after the ceremony—before to wash off any evil spirits and after to wash away any sacred residue.

An interesting aspect of hands is the number of beliefs that have grown up around them, only a few of which are included here. Countless superstitions, magical and religious rites have involved the hands and fingers, as if humans were always on the search for new signs and symbolic gestures for the initiated.

HEAD

The head has also been of great importance in religious observances, as well as magical rites and common superstitions. An explanation is given by J. A. MacCulloch:

> Innumerable rites performed on or in connection with the head show the importance which is universally attached to it. As the uppermost member of the body, that which contains the organs of sight, hearing, taste, and smell, it is naturally much honoured; while, as containing such a vital organ as the brain, which, however, is connected with the process of thought mainly at comparatively late stages of civilization, it is regarded as a seat of life or of the soul. The head, with its many apertures—nose, mouth, ears, sutures of skull—is a chief spirit-entry, either for a divine spirit or a god (as in the process of inspiration) or for evil

spirits. In either case it must be carefully guarded. Hence among many savages and also in the higher culture the head is regarded as peculiarly sacred, and is the subject of many tabus.[1]

In certain South Seas tribes the head was so honored that women were not allowed to touch a man's head, and must never be above a man's head. The vulnerability of the head to evil led it to be covered or veiled against the entry of spirits. The ultimate dishonor was to a person's head, such as the Egyptians making footstools from the heads of slain enemies.

The deities of many religions are depicted with sun rays coming from their heads to show their divine power or with a nimbus (halo) in back of or surrounding the head. Hindu, Greek, Roman, Teutonic, and Slavic deities all have been depicted with the sun's rays emanating from their heads. Oriental heroes and saints, including Buddhists and Tibetans, have paralleled the Christian use of the nimbus.

Because of the importance of the head to humans, it figured that the gods would often be shown with more than one head. The Indian Brahma has four heads. The Celtic god of the underworld had multiple heads. The Greek Geryon had three heads, the Hydra nine heads, and the giants of Norse mythology up to nine hundred heads. Although the Egyptians and Semites were not apt to show multiheaded gods, the Christians did use such representations for the Trinity.

Primitive tribes often wore the heads of animals in their religious ceremonies, such as American Indians wearing the heads of buffaloes and imitating their movements to assure good hunting. The Celts, Teutons, and many other cultures wore the heads of goats, cats, dogs, or deer, or sometimes masks representing the animal. Many religions represented their deities in a combined form, often using the head of the animal and the body of a man or woman. Egypt had many gods with animal heads. Pan had a goat's horns and ears,

Monks' Skulls

The heads of holy men were often thought to possess special powers, even after death. Skulls in a Greek monastery.

James J. Stanfield/National Geographic Image Collection, Washington, D.C.

Demeter a horse's head, Ganesa in India an elephant's head. In other religions the head remained human, but part or all of the body became animal, such as the Egyptian Sphinx, often the winged Christian angels, and the Babylonian winged bulls.

Taking the head as a war trophy is a familiar concept; it shows the prowess of the warrior and at the same time dishonors the enemy. Babylonian and Assyrian warriors left their enemies unburied and, as a further insult and impediment to their ghosts, cut off their heads. Artistic representations often show headless corpses at the foot of gods, or vultures flying off with severed heads. Egyptian kings are shown holding a cluster of heads, and the Hebrews have severed heads being brought to Gideon, David cutting off Goliath's head, the Philistines cutting off Saul's head, and so on. The Celts sometimes piled the heads of victims to count the dead. Some ninety thousand heads formed a pyramid on the ruins of Baghdad. Trophies also included parts of the head; sacks were filled with ears; mouths were worn as bracelets; noses and ears were worn as necklaces by the Arabs. And we are told that the Christian emperor Constantine gratefully accepted a plate of noses as an offering.

Heads are frequently preserved and displayed on poles or in sacred locations. Where headhunters are involved, they suppose that the strength of their victims or their ghosts will accrue to the owner. The Irish, for example, believed that milk drunk from a skull would restore a warrior's power.

Similar beliefs are found in current religions, indicating the primitive origin of many contemporary ideas:

> In the Christian Church, among the relics of saints or martyrs the head or skull has frequently been singled out for adoration or as possessing great miraculous power. Thus "the head of Saint Marnan, preserved at Aberchirder, was ceremonially washed every Sunday, and the water carried to the sick and diseased, who derived benefit and recovered health from its sanative properties." Among Muhammadans a similar reverence is paid; e.g., the burial-place of the head of al-Husain in Cairo is much visited by worshipers.[2]

Many religious rites involve the head. The laying on of hands frequently uses the head as the point of contact; anointing and baptism involve the head. The head is often shaved so that evil spirits cannot cling to it; Egyptians, Indians, and Arabs often shaved the heads of babies for this reason. The Chinese hoped that by shaving the baby's head the evil spirits would mistake the infant for a Buddhist monk and stay clear. A number of priesthoods, such as the Buddhists, shave their heads; the tonsure of the Christian Church is also a way to protect against evil spirits. Apart from the hair, magicians and priests frequently cover their heads during ceremonies to avoid any impurities or spirits that might be present, or simply as a show of respect for the divinity. The ancient priests usually covered their heads and the Jews and Muhammadans adopted coverings. Saint Paul taught that Christian men should not dishonor their heads by praying covered, but he insisted that Christian women cover theirs. Christians, Jews, and Muhammadans have at times insisted that brides or women in general wear veils to protect the head, and particularly at the time of marriage.

There is, then, a great universality of custom in honoring the head and in protecting the head from evil influences. Most of these religious beliefs have been passed down through the ages.

PHALLUS

Another part of the body that has been worshiped by many is the phallus. To many primitive people the phallus symbolized generative power which was, at best, a mysterious force and not well understood. Thus in the early display of phallic symbols and their worship, there was no obscenity intended but only recognition that people were dependent on their reproductive powers to continue as a family or a people. In some cases where ancestors were worshiped, the ancestor was represented in ithyphallic form (an erect penis), as it was supposed that he had not only the power but a particular interest in continuing his line.

Earlier and indigenous cultures assumed that the principles of imitative magic applied in the case of reproduction, so where the people were dependent on a certain animal for food they would conduct a ceremony designed to assist that animal to reproduce. For example, a tribe on the coast of Brazil lived mainly on fish, and conducted a ceremony in which a man was masked as a dolphin with an oversized phallus; his actions were supposed to encourage the impregnation of dolphins. In like manner, in some areas of Java, husband and wife would run naked around the rice field and end in an embrace which they hoped would encourage the rice to blossom more abundantly. In another island culture, if the clove crop were threatened, the man went by night to the plantation and there in his naked state simulated coition with one of the trees while crying "more cloves!" These and other examples show the applications of imitative magic to agriculture, where growing crops were regarded as living things which, it was believed, could be aroused to a sexual excitement.

Nakedness alone was thought to have an effect on the elements. Pliny reported that a woman undressing herself in nature was a deterrent to storms. In Southern India, when incessant rains threatened to flood the fields, naked men stood under the sky beating their drums and pointing firebrands toward heaven; their nudity was supposed to shock and scandalize the spirits that cause rain and therefore encourage their departure. In some Saxon settlements in Transylvania, the farmer would walk nude through the fields before sunrise to prevent birds from eating the new seed; he ended his journey by saying a Paternoster.

There have been many cures for barrenness that involved an image of the phallus. The Dharwar women of India would go from house to house carrying an image called Jokamar whose external genitalia were several times larger than the rest of his body; in return for singing Jokamar's praises the householder rewarded the woman with a small present. At Roman weddings the bride was supposed to sit on an idol of Priapus, a god of fertility and son of Aphrodite, goddess of love. The god Upsala, in what is now

Sweden, was represented with a large phallus and was worshiped at weddings with various sacrifices. An unusual practice was found in Java:

> On the island of Java, at Batavia, an old and useless cannon, lying in a field, was regarded by the natives as a divinity in phallic form, and daily worshiped with offerings of rice and fruit, miniature sunshades, and coppers. It was held to cure sterility in women, for which purpose it was necessary to sit astride on it for some time. Women might be seen—sometimes two at once—dressed in their best and adorned with flowers, doing this at any period of the day. For years the priests encouraged the practice, to their own pecuniary benefit, until at length the cannon was removed by the Dutch Government.[3]

Ancient civilizations had their own customs and cures revolving around the phallus. Herodotus describes how every Babylonian woman was required to prostitute herself at least once with a stranger—the first man at the temple to throw a silver coin in her lap. A number of cultures dedicated girls to become prostitutes at the temple of a divinity whose specialty was fertility; this seems to have been a feature of the cult of an Armenian goddess and there may have been indications that sacred prostitution was also known in the worship of Yahweh. In a related custom, there was a practice among some people in India whereby a barren wife was subjected to the embraces of one or more strangers, all in the hope of becoming pregnant.

Egypt had more than one god of fertility, but Osiris was the chief god of vegetation and the creator of life. His representation was said to include a large phallus, and Herodotus relates how on festival days Egyptian women carried his image—about eighteen inches in length with a phallus almost as large, which operated on strings. The Greeks identified Osiris with their own god Dionysus and prominently displayed his phallus in orgiastic rites which saw sacrificial victims torn in pieces and eaten raw; the participants indulged in sexual intercourse along with wild dancing and wine. These rites of Dionysus were all thought to result from possession by the god and therefore the participants were blameless and not thought to have lost their modesty.

Rome, too, had excesses in the Bacchanalia which finally resulted in suppression by the Roman Senate. It appears, in fact, that throughout medieval Europe fertility rites of this sort were not uncommon, particularly in the spring to commemorate the revival of the land from its wintry grasp.

In the Middle Ages, and since, various parts of France and Belgium are known to have worshiped ithyphallic saints to obtain children or cure impotency. Saint Foutin, the traditional first bishop of Lyons, was one whose worship was widespread; when the Protestants took over in 1585, "they found among the sacred relics of the principal church an object said to be his phallus. Its extremity was reddened by the libations of wine offered to it by women in need of his help."[4]

In Provence during the sixteenth century wax models of sex organs were suspended from the ceiling of a chapel dedicated to Saint Foutin, and it is said they were so numerous that when the wind stirred they bumped against each other to the distraction of the devoted. Women who wished husbands or children were known to rub against phallic representations which included stones, trees of a suggestive appearance, or statues of saints known for their assistance in these respects.

In England a number of phallic images were found, including the 180-foot figure of the nude Cerne giant, whose body with exaggerated sexual organs was cut in the turf in Dorset. Irish churches in the Middle Ages sometimes contained female effigies with exaggerated sex organs; they were known as Sheila-na-gig.

Some Italian churches sold waxen effigies of various parts of the body, although the trade was overwhelmingly done in phalli, mostly purchased by the women. Inside the church the supplicant presented himself or herself to the priest and exposed the part of their body afflicted, which was then anointed with the consecrated "oil of Saint Cosmas." After a time, Ecclesiastical legislation prescribed a penance of bread and water during three Lents for incantations made to a phallus.

In Greece and Rome, cakes were made in phallic shapes for weddings or ceremonies relating to firstfruits. Even in the twentieth century, the figure of a phallus is among the most common amulets worn in Italy and many Mediterranean countries, where it is regarded as protection against witchcraft and particularly the evil eye of sorcerers. Victorious Italian generals were said to have a phallic image before their cars as they entered Rome in triumphant procession.

The size of the phallus was exaggerated, but not necessarily with any obscene intent. As hands were considered a symbol of power, many gods were given extra hands or arms to denote their strength; in the same way, some gods were given many heads to denote great intelligence. The oversized phallus was in many cases a representation of the power of the god with respect to fertility.

So images of the phallus were often used in both magical and religious rites. In many cultures the phallus came to represent more than the generative power of men—it signified the creative power of nature, and as such could ward off the evil eye, sterility, and death.

It should come as no surprise that phallic worship was an important part of many indigenous cultures. Sex was a mysterious thing, and whenever something could not be explained in rational terms it was often assigned to the world of magic or the world of spirits. The worship of the phallus remained a part of human religious observances for a long time; eventually the sexual element was to influence religious beliefs in a variety of ways, including such aberrant behavior as extreme asceticism.

NOTES

1. James Hastings, ed., "Head," *The Encyclopaedia of Religion and Ethics* (New York: Charles Scribner and Sons, 1951), p. 532.

2. Ibid., p. 536.

3. Ibid., "Phallism," p. 820.

4. Ibid., p. 817.

19

The Soul:
An Inner Man and Woman

he idea of a soul had its origin when primitive humans tried to explain the life force—the force that was present in a living body, but absent in a dead body. They concluded that the invisible and intangible difference must be attributable to an unseen spirit, or soul, that occupied the living body. Their reasoning also led them to suppose that the bigger man must be powered by a little man inside his body and that animals were likewise powered by an internal beast of smaller stature. The little man, the little animal, was the soul.

So along with the idea of a soul, primitive humans did their best to envision it. In many cases the human soul was thought to be an exact replica of the individual, although about the size of a thumb and somewhat incorporeal, which permitted it to move about within the body. The invisible and insubstantial nature of the soul also permitted the soul to leave the body; sleep was considered a temporary absence of the soul and death a permanent absence.

In order to encourage the soul's return when a person's health or disposition suggested their soul was wandering, some ancients scattered rice in an appeal to its appetite. Other stratagems were in place to keep the soul in the body of a corpse, lest the body go to its reward unaccompanied by its spirit. As most escapes were made through the nose and mouth, the soul was often contained by plugging the nose or binding the mouth.

The absence of the soul from the body was always risky business because the soul might be exposed to baleful influences in its travels. There were, however, safeguards that could be employed to protect the disengaged soul, even for an indefinite period. The indigenes viewed the soul as a material object, capable of being lifted, placed in a box or jar, and hidden from view; in this condition the soul might still be of use to the individual as the principles of sympathetic magic would apply. So even from a distance the soul could work its good on the body, or alternatively could adversely affect the body if its safety was compromised. For this reason, great care was taken to deposit the soul in a snug place where it would be secure. Indeed, on the occasion of a great battle natives would sometimes disengage their souls and leave them in the safety of their home.

Throughout ancient civilizations there are stories about how souls were secreted but later found by an adversary, much to the chagrin of the original owner. Security arrangements might include placing the soul in a box within a box, burying it beneath a tree, and assigning the tree and assorted demons the role of protecting the soul from sorcerers.

Trees were, in fact, often supposed to possess a soul that would bear a sympathetic relationship to the human soul. Some societies planted a seed each time a child was born and it was assumed that, as the tree grew straight and strong, so would the child. Should the branches wither and the tree die, however, it was assumed that a similar misfortune would befall the child.

The interaction between plant and human souls was also believed possible between animal and human souls. In particular, wizards were believed to have two souls and to keep one of them in an animal, both to secure the powers of that animal to themselves and also to keep a soul in reserve should ill fortune befall their embodied soul. As might be expected, the most powerful wizards had concealed their second, or external souls, in the more ferocious animals and high-flying birds. Stories from the past relate how wizards often battled by sending forth their external souls in the bodies of fierce beasts before they themselves joined in the encounter. Witches also contracted mystic alliances with birds or beasts wherein lodged their souls.

So, in the animistic view, there was complete democracy in the concept of soul. Everything "dignified by thinghood" had its own power or function and therefore its own soul—the idea of a soul was not restricted to humans or animate objects.

Nor has there been a necessary limit on the number of souls a person might possess. The Caribs believed that one soul resided in the head, another in the heart, and still others wherever the blood could be felt to pulsate. Other societies somewhat arbitrarily believed that people had four souls, each of which could sustain their body—but after the fourth soul had departed they must die. The natives of Laos count a total of thirty spirits or souls that reside in the body, fairly well covering all of the vital and functioning parts.

Some ancient civilizations, such as Egypt, had quite elaborate ideas about the soul. In Egypt, both gods and humans were thought to possess souls which were the source of all power and strength. The preferred way of depicting the soul was as a heron, and in later times the soul was represented as a heron with a human face, allowing relatives to place a likeness of the departed's face on the body of a bird. The Egyptian soul was thought to wander around the desert or elsewhere during the day but, of need, return to the body at night where it would be safe from attacks by evil spirits—this may have led the Egyptians to preserve the body for as long as possible through mummification. Also important to the spirits of the deceased were the foods, possessions, and servants enjoyed by the spirits while alive; beer, concubines, and other items for the gratification of desires were included. Earlier beliefs that the Egyptian spirits stayed in the tomb were extended to allow a place in the sky and "sometimes a little ladder or a boat was pictured, by which the soul could climb or sail away to the stars." On a more somber note, the ancient Egyptians eventually came to believe in a judgment day:

> In course of time it came to be believed that on its arrival in the underworld the soul must undergo an examination to see whether it was fit to go to heaven. While Osiris was believed to be the great judge, he was attended by 42 assessors—one for each of Egypt's nomes. These bore such terrifying names as "Blood-Drinker," "Bone-Breaker," "Shadow-Swallower." Those who successfully passed the examination and could say at the end, "I am pure," were transferred to the sky, where they enjoyed a material paradise such as was, in the Pyramid Texts, the lot of kings. These promises were only for the worthy. The wicked were doomed to destruction by the myriads of demons who inhabited the underworld. They might be torn in pieces by the forty-two terrible judges, burned in furnaces, or drowned in the abyss. These souls might themselves become demons and return to torment the living with disease and death. Against them, as against other demons, magic spells were necessary.[1]

An interesting addition to the Egyptian concept of a soul was the concept of a ka, or double. The ka was a corporeal, although invisible, comrade who accompanied a person through life and preceded them to heaven to arrange for their reception before Osiris.

The Egyptians serve as an example of a civilization that had rather definite ideas about the soul, and acted out their lives and deaths accordingly. There was also a common belief among the ancients that the soul or spirit of a person or animal was in the blood. Thus *The Golden Bough* relates that some Estonians would not taste animal blood because it was thought to contain the animal's soul, and that by eating the blood the soul of the animal would enter the body of the person. For the same reason some North American Indian tribes rejected the idea of eating an animal's blood. Jewish hunters spilled the blood of animals on the ground and covered it with dirt, believing that the soul of the animal was in the blood and, presumably, should be buried—certainly not eaten. The blood of humans was also thought to contain the soul, and in the times of Kublai Khan or Marco Polo a person might be killed by strangulation, or beating, or even by being bounced inside a carpet to prevent their blood from being spilled, either because it was evil to destroy a person's soul or perhaps to prevent the desecration of royal blood by letting it touch the ground. There are instances of men being hired to lick the spilt blood of nobles to prevent their souls from falling into the hands of their enemies.

Blood, then, has been thought of as a conductor of the soul or more often as the soul itself. And the heart, in particular, was viewed as the seat of life or even as having a soul of its own. The concept of a "bleeding heart" has been a symbol of the soul in some religions. In part, the concept of sacrifice and the supposed blood lust of the spirit world is traceable to the idea that blood is, in fact, the soul or spirit:

> Finally, exsanguinate shades from the world below and gods in the heavens above alike delight in the odours of blood—in good sooth a spirit, which serves to invigorate their paler being. This is the blood of sacrifice and the blood of atonement, which is, in

Ascending Soul

The soul of a dying man issues from his mouth as angels and demons vie for it. From a drawing in the early 1800s.

J. Collin de Plancy, *Dictionnaire Infernal.* Mary Evans Picture Library, London.

fact, the blood of life. The most astonishing of all developments of this idea was that of the Aztec, who believed that the sun is maintained in its course and the world in its order solely by the unceasing effluvia of human blood drenching altars and shrines. Nor is there any idea more ubiquitous in literature than that of blood symbolism.[2]

So, from early peoples up to the present there have been infinite variations on the concept of a soul. The most basic concepts include the embodied spirit which gives life to the body, the disembodied spirit which is free to wander, and the ghosts, or doubles, of the departed. Within these basic concepts religions have chosen their preferred view of the soul, changed it according to need, and embellished it with a number of innovative and unique aspects. But there are few, if any, modern conceptions of the soul that are not found in the beliefs of ancient civilizations or even earlier humankind. We may not undertake, as the Egyptians did, to place a little ladder or boat in the tomb so that the soul could climb or sail its way to the stars; but we share other Egyptian beliefs about the soul including a day of judgment wherein the pure soul is rewarded and the tainted soul punished in eternal fires. At whatever points modern and ancient humans may choose to agree or disagree on the nature of the soul, it would be difficult to fault their respective conclusions based on considerations of evidence.

The lack of evidence for the existence of a soul, and perhaps the primitive reasoning that prompted the idea, have led to disbelief among most scientists. On the other hand, most theologians accept the idea of an immortal soul.

All cultures and civilizations have chosen to speculate on the existence of a soul and in time have reached a working conclusion. In the presence of an unfathomable mystery, humans have chosen to have their own understanding of the phenomena, rather than live in a state of perpetual wonder. But the origin of the idea is clear: the concept of a soul was an attempt by minds of earlier times to explain the life force—the invisible force that gives life to our bodies. Humans explained this mystery of nature, as they did other natural phenomena, by attributing it to an unseen spirit, or soul.

Finally, the concept of a soul separable from the body allows humans to have their dream of life everlasting. The body comes to an end, but the soul is presumed to live forever. This possibility is clearly welcome in a society that is concerned with death and governed above all else by a will to survive. If the body cannot continue beyond a given number of years, there is some satisfaction in believing that the soul lives forever.

The acceptance of the idea of a soul is aided immeasurably, then, by our desire to overcome the natural law, or death. And given the circumstance that the existence of a soul has been neither proved nor disproved, it is no surprise that one may choose to believe his or her spirit will enjoy life everlasting. Indeed, some religions promise that both body and soul will survive, a condition which would fully satisfy a desire to live forever, although not all humans share that desire.

NOTES

1. James Hastings, ed., "Soul," *The Encyclopaedia of Religion and Ethics* (New York: Charles Scribner and Sons, 1951), p. 756.

2. Ibid., p. 726.

20

An Afterlife:
The Impossible Dream

*T*he concept of resurrection began when early people ruminated over the change of seasons. Seasonal changes were a source of wonder and were also intimately connected with their survival; the earth's vegetation died and later in the year came back to life—a resurrection. Humans and animals also came to be thought of as part of this eternal process, and so vegetable, animal, and human were all joined in a restoration or rejuvenation concept attributed to the gods.

One such god was Osiris, whose death and resurrection were celebrated as early as 1500 B.C.E. Osiris was the most popular of the Egyptian gods and governed many aspects of life, including the sun, fertility, vegetation, and especially corn. Before Osiris, myth says, the ancient Egyptians had been cannibals, but Osiris introduced them to the possibilities of agriculture. He was the first to gather fruit from the trees, to teach vines how to climb a pole, and to tread on grapes. In an unfortunate and very involved conspiracy,

Osiris was killed by a jealous brother, his body torn into fourteen pieces and scattered around the land. Finally the sun-god Ra sent help from heaven in the form of Anubis, the jackal-headed god. The broken body of Osiris was then reassembled and wrapped in linen bandages. When he recovered, Osiris became Ruler of the Dead and judged the souls of humans after hearing their confessions. The Egyptians took the resurrection to mean that they enjoyed a similar opportunity, provided that their funerals were conducted in a manner consistent with the rebirth of Osiris; therefore the human dead received the same treatment as Osiris, including the linen bandages that we associate with mummies. Although Osiris was resurrected, he did not resume his earthly life, but instead ascended into heaven.

The resurrection of gods was not limited to Egypt. The Greek god Dionysus, or Bacchus, was also torn to pieces by jealous gods but also came back to life with the help of Zeus and Apollo. Dionysus, too, had responsibilities in agriculture, particularly the grape—which may account for much of his popularity among Greek worshipers. In some rituals in his honor, worshipers tore live animals apart with their teeth, in acknowledgement of the nature of Dionysus's own death by dismemberment.

Other Greek deities to share in the resurrection idea were Demeter and Persephone, mother and daughter. It seems that Persephone was picking wildflowers when she was kidnapped by Pluto, lord of the dead, and taken to his gloomy underworld. Demeter, a corn-goddess with yellow tresses, refused to let the corn grow until her daughter had been restored to her, and once again Zeus intervened. Persephone was required to spend the winter months with her husband in the nether world, but in the spring of each year rejoined her mother, which was fortunate for those interested in the corn crop.

Still another resurrected god was Adonis, who was worshiped by the Semitic peoples of Babylonia and Syria. The Greeks followed and worshiped the god as early as the seventh century B.C.E. Adonis was the god of vegetation and, in particular, corn. As one would expect, his passing occurred in the fall of each year and his resurrection in the spring. In Egypt and Phoenicia as well, Adonis died annually but then came back to life and ascended into heaven in the presence of his worshipers. The religious rites that celebrated the death and resurrection of Adonis were very much a part of the culture of the time, and Frazer suggests an adaptation of the rite: "When we reflect how often the church has skillfully contrived to plant the seeds of the new faith on the old stock of paganism, we may surmise that the Easter celebration of the dead and risen Christ was grafted upon a similar celebration of the dead and risen Adonis."[1]

The death and resurrection of Attis also may have a special significance for Christianity. He also appeared to be a god of vegetation. The birth of Attis was said to be miraculous and his mother, Nana, a virgin. Sir James Frazer notes that tales about virgin births were "relics of an age of childlike ignorance when men had not yet recognized the intercourse of the sexes as the true cause of offspring." Attis can be dated to about 200 B.C.E.

When Attis died each year, a period of mourning took place, but this was followed by a joyous celebration:

> The sorrow of the worshipers was turned to joy. For suddenly a light shone in the darkness: the tomb was opened: the god has risen from the dead; and as the priest touched the lips of the weeping mourners with balm, he softly whispered in their ears the glad tidings of salvation. The resurrection of the god was hailed by his disciples as a promise that they too would issue triumphant from the corruption of the grave. On the morrow, the twenty-fifth day of March, which was reckoned the vernal equinox, the divine resurrection was celebrated with a wild outburst of glee.[2]

Christ's Resurrection

Detail of Piero della Francesca's painting of Christ rising triumphant from the tomb, thereby offering all Christians the hope of eternal life.

Courtesy of Museo Civico, Sansepolcro, Italy.

As it happened, the resurrection of Christ paralleled rather closely the resurrection of Attis, which gave pause to the worshipers of that time:

> In point of fact it appears from the testimony of an anonymous Christian, who wrote in the fourth century of our era, that Christians and pagans alike were struck by the remarkable coincidence between the death and resurrection of their respective deities, and that the coincidence formed a theme of bitter controversy between the adherents of the rival religions, the pagans contending that the resurrection of Christ was a spurious imitation of the resurrection of Attis, and the Christians asserting with equal warmth that the resurrection of Attis was a diabolical counterfeit of the resurrection of Christ. In these unseemly bickerings the heathen took what to a superficial observer might seem strong ground by arguing that their god was the older and therefore presumably the original, not the counterfeit, since as a general rule an original is older than its copy. This feeble argument the Christians easily rebutted. They admitted, indeed, that in point of time Christ was the junior deity, but they triumphantly demonstrated his real seniority by falling back on the subtlety of Satan, who on so important an occasion had surpassed himself by inverting the usual order of nature.[3]

Actually, many Christian festivals had their origin in heathen rites. The celebration of Easter corresponds with the resurrection of Attis, who combined a divine father and divine son in his person. Christmas is celebrated on the day of Mithra's nativity as the newborn sun. The festival of Saint George in April replaced the pagan festival of Parilia; the festival of the Assumption of the Virgin in August replaced the festival of Diana; the feast of All Souls' Day in November was a continuation of an ancient heathen feast of the dead.

Apart from gods, the concept of a resurrection of the human

body had been established in Judaism in the second century B.C.E. The idea was then inherited by Christianity and Islam. All three religions believe in a literal reanimation of the physical body.

Reincarnation is similar to the concept of resurrection, as it promises a life after death. Reincarnation supposes that after death the spirit lives on and passes through a succession of bodies. In other words, life is a cyclical process. The origin of reincarnation was probably a deduction made by early peoples. They saw birth and death and a family resemblance in children and supposed this meant that an ancestor had returned.

The idea of reincarnation was recorded as early as 600 B.C.E. in India and became an integral part of Buddhism. It was also known in Greece in the sixth century B.C.E. and had its believers among the Celtics and the Teutonic religions.

Within Buddhism there are a number of variations on reincarnation, but the essential idea is the same. After death all should go to an underworld for judgment. Then the souls of the virtuous are reborn as gods; those who have lived a reasonably good life return to earth as men and women; sinners may be reborn as animals, hungry ghosts, or denizens of hell.

The six modes of Buddhist existence are depicted on a wheel: gods, demigods, human beings, animals, hungry ghosts, and demons. These six modes are then further subdivided into more closely defined categories still. The belief is that all beings are bound to the wheel, or cycle, of reincarnation until they attain release by attaining Buddhahood and Nirvana. The doctrine of reincarnation also became an integral part of Hinduism and Jainism. They differed somewhat from the beliefs of Buddhism, but all agree that there is a continuing self, which is reborn. They also agree that rebirth can lead to an improvement in status, with the eventual outcome of Moksha (release) for Hindus, in which the permanent self achieves union with Brahman.

Once again, the idea of a new life has its fascination for a society that is a continuing witness to death and the decay of the body. Both resurrection and reincarnation offer the hope of ever-lasting life and, better, the possibility of an improvement in one's circumstances in the hereafter. Indeed, the beliefs in a life to come often include sizable rewards for those who have kept the faith, and particularly for those who have sacrificed their lives for their religion. In some instances, exemplary conduct in this life may even lead to becoming a god in another incarnation.

So today resurrection and reincarnation address the dream to overcome death and live forever, although necessarily either in another environment or in another body. But many centuries ago, the concept of an afterlife began when early humans wondered about the change of seasons and the apparent death and rebirth of vegetation.

NOTES

1. Sir James G. Frazer, *The Golden Bough*, abridged ed. (New York: Macmillan Publishing Co., 1922), p. 401.

2. Ibid., p. 407.

3. Ibid., p. 419.

21

Summary:
Today's Religious Beliefs

THE ORIGIN OF RELIGIOUS BELIEFS

In ancient times, humans knew little about the nature of the universe. And for many ages natural phenomena could not be explained other than to suppose the presence of activating spirits—invisible beings who were much like humans in appearance and personality, but who were possessed of superhuman powers. When it was concluded that powerful spirits (gods) were in control of the universe, men and women could then explain all natural phenomena by a simple attribution to the spirit world. So a belief in spirits answered many questions about the universe at a time when science could not be called on for explanations.

Of course, the gods could be whatever humans wanted them to be; their unseen presence and unknown nature were proof against any revealed error on the part of the ancient authors. So the safeguards were in place for some noteworthy flights of fancy, and history records a panoply of gods and goddesses of varied description and disposition. There were corn-goddesses with golden tresses, cow-headed gods of Egyptian origin, Greek gods of surpassing personal beauty, bull-gods with impressive sexual powers, feathered serpents with a taste for blood, warrior-gods with a lust for battle, and storm-gods who controlled the elements. Whatever their particular appearance and penchant, they were usually characterized by a striking countenance and remarkable powers. And if the gods were somewhat overdrawn by modern standards, the authors may be forgiven their attempts to please an ancient and unsophisticated audience.

Today, we are the inheritors of these religious beliefs which began thousands of years ago. And only when we lift the veil can we see the strange and anomalous nature of many such beliefs. It is easier, of course, to observe that the beliefs of other religions often appear strange. For example:

- The Christian who looks with amusement at a Hindu god whose representation is half human and half elephant has no problem in accepting angels who have large, feathery wings.
- A Christian may marvel at the Indian belief that impurities of the soul may be rinsed off with the urine of a cow, although the Catholic baptismal ceremony once included the use of spittle.
- A Christian may smile at the native medicine man who gives (or sells) charms to ward off evil spirits, all the while wearing his or her own religious medal to ward off personal misfortune.

So we grow accustomed to ideas through continuous exposure, and the strange becomes familiar. And ideas that might appear bizarre or offensive outside of a religious context are easily accepted within the context of religion, where anything is possible.

Thus we are told about: the dead who have returned to life . . . virgins who have given birth . . . water that is turned into wine . . . sticks that are turned into snakes . . . men who can walk on water . . . diviners who read the future . . . humans who talk with gods . . . and, humans who are also gods.

Such beliefs as these must be accepted as a matter of faith, for they are not apparent within the realm of human experience. But they are, nonetheless, held as inviolable truth by the devout and, as some would point out, the nature of the claims is often such that they may be neither proved nor disproved. (Can one prove that a prophet does not talk with a god?)

And so the scientific community may regard such beliefs as unprovable hypotheses, or as good theatre, or put various other constructions on them. But science can not accept such beliefs as authenticated.

THE LEGACY OF THE ANCIENTS

Sigmund Freud had questioned current religious beliefs on several counts: "Criticism has whittled away the evidential value of religious documents, natural science has shown up the errors in them, and comparative research has been struck by the fatal resemblance between the religious ideas which we revere and the mental products of primitive peoples and times."[1] Modern scholarship has, indeed, traced the origin of today's religious beliefs to ancient civilizations and tribes:

Immortal Gods: The idea of gods—invisible spirits that orchestrate the universe—began in prehistoric times. Early humans attempted to explain the powerful forces of nature by the presence of activating spirits, and hoped that these same spirits would help them in their personal lives.

Human Gods: The belief in human gods began when certain individuals, on an unusual display of power, were accorded the status of gods. Human gods have been associated with many religions; traditionally, the founding figure of a religion has been proclaimed a human god.

Prophecy: Ancient prophets came to be recognized as spokespersons for gods when their aberrant behavior suggested they were possessed by spirits. Epilepsy, ecstatic trances, and hallucinogenic drugs have all provided the appearance of spiritual possession.

Holy Books: In early centuries, the Bible was viewed by Christians as the literal or inspired word of God and the ultimate authority on human affairs. Modern scholarship has revealed that many Bible narratives, such as the story of Genesis, were ancient myths and has noted inaccuracies and inconsistencies in the writings.

Prayer: Genetically, prayer came from the spells and incantations of the ancient magicians and merely substituted a request (religion) for a command (magic). The Christian belief that all of one's wishes will be granted is based on a brief biblical reference (Matt. 17:20).

Sacrifice: Although sacrifice is still a symbolic mainstay in many religions, it began as a primitive survival strategy: to satisfy the blood lust of the gods with somebody else's life. Some scholars link human sacrifice with the practice of cannibalism.

Miracles: Religions around the world have used miracles as supposed proof that their gods possess supernatural powers and can therefore offer protection from the natural phenomena. Miracles are the common stock of primitive religious beliefs.

Communion: Communion had its roots in sympathetic magic, wherein early people believed that a person absorbed the qualities of the animal, human, or god that they consumed. Prior to Christianity, a number of ancient religions concluded that bread and wine could be transformed into the body and blood of a god.

Baptism: The rite of baptism traces back to early peoples who saw the cleansing power of water and supposed that evil spirits could be washed away in the same manner as dirt. Later the concept was expanded to include washing away the enervating effects of sin and moral guilt.

Circumcision: Circumcision was one of several mutilations of the sexual organs that were widespread among early peoples. Some attribute circumcision to a preoccupation with sex; others to an expression of adult dominance over children and the young.

Exorcism: The Christian rite of exorcism began with early peoples who believed that evil spirits could inhabit a person's body; the evidence of possession was any action or attitude that seemed uncharacteristic of the person. Demonic possession is now recognized as a mistaken interpretation of mental and physical ailments.

Asceticism: Asceticism began with the Dionysian cult in Greece and the attempt to achieve ecstasy by freeing the soul from the body. Christianity adopted the idea as a way to rid the body of demons while accepting a deserved punishment for sin. Extreme asceticism is now recognized as a form of masochism.

The Body: Hands, heads, and phalli have all been revered by religions and countless rites have grown up around them. The rites are accounted for by the ancient beliefs in sympathetic magic, wherein the body relic of a saint, for example, is thought to have continuing powers.

The Soul: The concept of a soul had its origin among early humans who concluded that the life force—the energy present in a living body but absent in a dead body—must be an unseen spirit (a soul). Later, the idea of a soul that was separable from the body allowed humans the hope of an everlasting life.

An Afterlife: The idea of an afterlife began when early people wondered about the change of seasons and the apparent death and rebirth of vegetation. The resurrection of Attis, a vegetation-god, was the direct forbear of the Christian idea of resurrection, although many resurrection stories preceded Christianity.

Finally, scholars have shown that many of our current religious beliefs are neither original nor exclusive. Christian religious beliefs are, for the most part, adaptations of earlier beliefs whose origins were rooted in ancient or even prehistoric cultures.

Religion may see the wisdom of the ages in the longevity of these beliefs and a commonality among cultures that suggests an inborn or divinely inspired religious tendency. But science sees a different picture—an ancient and unsophisticated audience whose beliefs arose from wishful thinking and mistaken ideas about natural phenomena and were perpetuated by a vigorous religious tradition.

THE NATURE OF SUPERSTITION

For many centuries the Christian religion offered to explain the nature of the universe, and did so by attributing all unknown events to a spirit world whose inhabitants circled high above, or lurked in unseen depths, from where they could cause good fortune or ill for the peoples of the world. It was suggested that the Church alone could provide an understanding of the great mysteries of the natural world and offer protection from the unknown forces that affect the human race.

And still today, the innocents of each new generation venture into the world with an accumulation of religious beliefs that began thousands of years ago among primitive peoples given over to their superstitions. *Webster* defines superstition as: "A belief or practice resulting from ignorance, fear of the unknown, trust in magic or chance, or a false conception of causation."

So many begin their Christian lives with an angel as their guardian, someone to protect them against any misfortune that might come along. And this same guardian angel is only the beginning of many beliefs:

- We believe that water will rinse away the enervating effects of sin, and demons.
- We wear amulets around our necks to ward off accidents and personal misfortune.
- We believe that certain gestures of the hand can bestow blessings on ourselves and others.
- We trust the symbol of a cross, however wrought, to bless and protect our beings.
- We know of towns, or walls, or waters with mystical healing powers not found elsewhere.
- We believe that the touch of a priest's hand will restore health to our bodies.
- We believe the dead can aid the living and ask their plaster likenesses for help.
- We believe that body parts of the dead, when preserved, have powers to protect the living.
- We believe that certain words, said in a given sequence, can call down spirits from above.
- We suppose that the incantations of a priest can cause the devil to depart our bodies.
- We assume that the repetition of a prayer will increase its efficacy, in some proportion to the count.
- We believe that by debasing our bodies we can in some way energize our immortal souls.

- We eat the flesh and drink the blood of a man-god—it once was bread and wine.
- We believe that consuming a man-god will make us holier, even godlike in some respects.
- And we believe in ghosts, in good and bad fairies, and in invisible beings that control our lives.

The explanation for such superstitious beliefs has been identified by Freud as merely wishful thinking. We wish to believe that a religious medal will protect us from harm, that a priest's touch will restore our health, that relics from the dead have marvelous powers—and so we do believe. It is an appealing idea, that help is available and that we have the means to access such help. Of course it is a vain wish, but, like prayer, we choose to believe a superstition in the absence of more certain assistance. We pray when the doctor offers us no hope, not when the doctor assures us that a cure is available, painless, and free of risk. So the "wishful thinking" that Freud identified is probably the source of many of our superstitions.

There is another aspect of human nature that encourages a belief in superstition. Each of us is born with an innate curiosity about cause and effect, for without such curiosity we would be unable to explain the world around us and adapt to its complexities. As an individual and as a society we probe our surroundings to understand our environment and to benefit as a result. In a word, the process is called *science*. Through every generation the child asks "why," which is the scientist in all of us searching for answers and the means to control our destiny. Superstition attempts to serve the same function as science, by claiming the ability to control events, but of course the claims are false. Superstition is largely based on hearsay and offers no validation for its claims, asking that they be accepted as a matter of belief. As it happens, those who wear a religious amulet seldom ask for proof of its effectiveness.

Superstition, of course, is more characteristic of cultures where education has not revealed the true nature of things. We are not apt to worship the god of the volcano after volcanologists from the local university have explained the phenomenon. We are less apt to pray for rain when we realize that our pastors, priests and popes have no control over the elements. And, overall, the existence of a spirit world is less credible when we begin to realize that it is not spirits that take care of us, but ourselves. There comes a time when we realize that the local doctor takes care of our illnesses, not the intercession of saints. The judge we went to school with dispenses justice, not an arbiter from above. A general from West Point defends our country, not a flight of angels. And superstition eventually gives way to the reality of our existence and our dependence on other humans.

All faiths give form and substance to invisible spirits that are supposed to control humankind. Whether the spirit is a god, demon, or one of the many other creatures that are said to inhabit this universe, it is given a name, face, and nature which then allows a relationship to begin. One can not relate to a nameless, faceless, and formless being whose nature remains a mystery. And the improvisations by the clergy have been noteworthy, ranging from the feathered serpents of some South American cultures to the winged horses and goatish personalities of some European and Middle Eastern cultures. The characters represented by the Greek and Roman deities, in fact, were more real in appearance and personality than most of the religious figures before or since.

The Irish serve as an example of a country that has given the world many colorful personages of superstitious origin. From Ireland we have sprites, elves, leprechauns, fairies, banshees, goblins—an altogether generous assortment of figures from an Irish spirit world.

Christianity has done no less and counts among its religious figures ghosts, witches, dragons, angels, imps, devils, and demons of various configurations to meet the varied circumstances of Christian living. The Christian roster is not unlike that of other religions, of course, all of which are rich in improbable personalities. Still, these figures from a fantasy world were vouched for by the Church and feared and revered by the Christian faithful. So Michael, the archangel, with his mighty wings and sword, did battle with the fallen angel, Lucifer, who favored a red outfit cut to accommodate his horns and pointy tail. (No one has ever explained why Lucifer fell from grace, so in theatrical terms one might conclude that the costuming was good but the plot was weak.)

Sooner or later such fanciful creations recede from the real world and become recognized as myth, as did the Greek gods and goddesses and the impressive array of Irish apparitions. In the meantime, the credibility of all Christian beliefs must suffer from an association with an ancient and bizarre spirit world.

NOTE

1. Sigmund Freud, *The Future of an Illusion* (New York: W. W. Norton and Company, 1961), p. 38.

Epilogue

The natural tendency of men and women to hope for the best is one reason for the perpetuation of religious beliefs. As Freud pointed out, it is more than mere coincidence that religion promises to make our every dream come true. We are offered powers over natural phenomena, protection from our enemies, safeguards against accidents and illness, and even peeks into the future. We are also offered consolation when the aforementioned dreams never quite seem to work out. And further, religion promises that even death is only an illusion and that eternal life awaits us. It is a formidable offering to those who live their lives in suffering and insecurity and who are governed above all else by a will to survive.

So the promises of religion answer every human wish and are aimed at our most basic drive—the will to survive. This is the power of religious beliefs: they offer a ready-made solution for an imperfect world and an impermanent existence. The longing for religious beliefs to be true, however, could not guarantee their per-petuation for as long as they have endured, were it not for the rein-forcement and support they have received from tradition and the authority of the Church.

Some of the aboriginal tribes of Australia, for example, still recite religious stories that reflect a considerable age—scholars wonder if the stories may date back to the Ice Age or earlier, for the archeological evidence indicates they first arrived in Australia some sixty thousand years ago. One of the elders of the tribe explained how their religious traditions were sustained from gen-eration to generation: he recalled, as a boy, sitting in a circle for religious instruction and being poked in the rear end with a spear when his mind wandered. This assured his attention to the busi-ness at hand.

There are more sophisticated assurances today. As one example, a Catholic at the turn of the last century was introduced to the faith when a babe in arms. The milestones of his or her life—birth, marriage, death—were all associated with religious ceremonies. Formal religious instruction began as a child in cate-chism class and perhaps continued in Catholic schools. Prayers were said morning and evening, and before and after meals—eight reminders a day. Religious holidays, feast days, and fast days marked all of the seasons, culminating in the extended Christmas and Easter observances.

Adherence to Catholic ideals was assured by censorship of certain books and movies and also by bans on music composers whose private lives were held to be objectionable. Marriage to another Catholic was mandatory unless a special exemption was granted, in which case the non-Catholic partner was required to take instruction and bring the children up as Catholics. Discipline was maintained by requirements of confession and penance, and the prospect of punishment both in this life and in the hereafter. Excommunication was a possibility; in its milder form excommunication involved the sacraments being withheld, in its harsher form the unfortunate was cursed with bell, book, and candle. Above all, the pressure to conform and to believe came from family, friends, teachers, priests, and a society which scorned—and often persecuted—unbelievers. It was more than a poke in the rear end with a spear.

There are several characteristics of today's religious beliefs that deserve consideration. The first is the exclusivity of the beliefs and benefits claimed by every religion. The second is the infallibility claimed by the religious leaders for their pronouncements. The third characteristic is what may be called the subjectivity of religious beliefs.

The Christian idea of exclusivity has been shared to a greater or lesser degree by all religions. Each religion has promoted its beliefs as the only authentic ones and claimed that its religion was uniquely favored by the gods. The ancients believed that their city was the center of the world, their planet the center of the universe, their god(s) the only true one(s), and their religion the only way to get to heaven where, by the way, the language spoken was their own.

Christianity also shared with other religions the prejudices that accompany a claim to exclusivity. Christians held that their religion was the only true religion and that the gods of other religions were false and probably fiendish in their origins and therefore were deserving of whatever prejudices came their way. So the concept of religious exclusivity created obstacles to human relations.

Catholics long proclaimed that only Catholics could go to heaven and that the faithful of other religions and even of other Christian denominations were doomed. This belief led Catholics to disparage members of other religions and, of course, caused resentment among the non-Catholic constituencies. Various other Christian denominations share this belief in exclusivity, and send missionaries and evangelists to "save" Catholics from damnation by converting them to "true" Christianity. Similarly, the supposition by Jews that they were "chosen" by God led to a similar feeling of exclusivity and superiority among the Jews and to anti-Semitic feelings among non-Jews who resented the arrogance of the claim.

By the twentieth century it has become apparent that claims of religious exclusivity are merely a function of human egos. Men and women like to believe that their cultural connections are superior to others, which by association reflects favorably on themselves. Religion simply brings more intensity to similar feelings about the superiority of one's country, city, neighborhood, club, team, family, and self.

However, claims of exclusivity in religion no longer have validity from a historical standpoint. Those who believe in the exclusivity of their religion must now contend with the fact that essentially the same religious beliefs were found to have been shared by many religions for thousands of years. Our Christian beliefs, for example, are neither original nor unique and can all be traced to more ancient religions and to primitive superstitions. So one may choose to believe that his or her Christian religious beliefs were implanted in an evolutionary process that affected Christians and non-Christians alike, but it is no longer possible to suppose that Christians were favored with insights that were unknown and unaccepted by other religions around the world. The idea of exclusivity is no longer credible.

The idea that holy books and religious leaders were infallible in their pronouncements was, of course, an idea proposed by the clergy. Authorities in other walks of life would also have people believe that they are incapable of error, and for the same reasons. However unreasonable, people are apt to believe in the infallibility of religious pronouncements because they would like to believe there is no margin for error in matters which could affect their immortal souls.

The Christian notions with respect to infallibility have centered on the Bible and the Roman Catholic pope. For the better part of two thousand years, Christians believed that the Bible was true in every respect and that any interpretations by the clergy were guided by the Holy Spirit. If the Muhammadans believed that the Quran was quite literally written by the angel Gabriel, the Christians were no less certain that the contents of the Bible were inspired and assured by the Supreme Being.

The authority of the Bible in all matters was vouchsafed by Saint Augustine in his famous pronouncement: "Nothing is to be accepted save on the authority of Scripture, since greater is that authority than all the powers of the human mind."[1] And so the presumed authority of the Bible carried into all fields of knowledge, including science.

As a consequence of a belief in the Bible as the infallible exposition of God's purposes and plans for the world, any other speculation seemed futile. Science, philosophy, and other inquiries into the human condition were abandoned or, if pursued, were carefully monitored by the ecclesiastical authorities for their compatibility with Holy Writ. Now the Bible is no longer thought to be infallible and its errors and inconsistencies are acknowledged by scientists and theologians alike. The origins of many Biblical stories are now known to be ancient myths and the authorship of other stories is now coming under question. So after many centuries we have been given permission to question the Bible.

As to the infallibility of the pope on matters of faith and morals, this assertion can perhaps be dismissed by remembering the number of popes who believed that church bells could change the weather. If further grist is needed for this mill, one may recall the Inquisition and similar events sanctioned by a succession of Roman Catholic popes.

So the concept of infallibility is no longer credible and the certainty that once marked Christian beliefs is now forfeit. Precepts that for centuries were unassailable given their source (the Bible or the pope) are now open to question. And to the extent that religious beliefs may no longer be explained or validated by an unquestionable authority, then the alternative is necessarily the exercise of reason. This appears to be the direction that Christianity is taking and it promises change.

With regard to subjectivity, the pride that many religions take in their vaunted exclusivity, and the support given that notion by the related claim of infallibility, have encouraged a subjective thought process. Religion has invited its members to accept church doctrine on faith alone. And clearly, religious beliefs, including the most fundamental, must be taken on faith, for there is no evidence, there are no proofs—beginning with a belief in the existence of God, carrying to the concept of divine intervention, including beliefs about baptism, exorcism, asceticism, and embracing the belief in a bodily resurrection and eternal life. The faithful, then, are aptly named.

So the religions of the world have each been pleased to address the unknown and formulate beliefs that explain the natural world and a life to come. Of course, such beliefs are wanting in objectivity, defined in Webster as "belonging to the sensible world and being observable or verifiable by scientific method." An example may be found in Bhutan, where Buddhists believe that the Guru Rimpoche arrived in the country on a flying tiger during the eighth century. Or a Christian who believes that messages from a spirit world are carried earthward by beings with birdlike wings. Throughout the world, religion has adorned its beliefs with the marvelous, with trappings that excite the imagination of the people and allow any one religion to stay competitive with the next. In fact, most religions have borrowed abundantly from the more ancient religions in compiling their registers of miracles.

Christianity has certainly followed suit with miracles that are both borrowed and wondrous: snakes that talk, virgins who give birth, men who walk on water, relics that repel demons, bread that becomes flesh, and men who become gods. One may, in fact, find most if not all of the Christian miracles first told by other religions in earlier times. Whether borrowed or not is perhaps less important than the circumstance that many Christians are still wedded to these early and improbable ideas.

The risk of carrying such beliefs into the twenty-first century is that the thoughtful may reject the core beliefs of Christianity because of their improbable accompaniments. At the least, such wondrous stories divert attention from the real business of religion—to encourage goodness among the people of the world. And it appears that, in fact, many Christian theologians are turning away from the miraculous tales of the ancients.

If miraculous happenings are set aside, there appear to be two focal points in religious beliefs. One deals with matters of self-interest and the other with matters of society.

In the beliefs that center on self-interest, each individual is promised that his or her welfare is of paramount importance to a powerful spirit or god. And this same spirit sees to it that their food source is maintained, their enemies thwarted, their health assured, their prayers answered, their sins forgiven, their bodies resurrected, and their souls preserved for ever and ever. Amen. So religion has assured the individual that his or her personal needs will be addressed, in ample fashion, in this world and the next. It has been an attractive if not compelling concept to most individuals— and understandably so.

The religious beliefs that center on individual self-interest, however, have little moral value inherent in them. The nature of these beliefs serves to attract a following, certainly, but religions' promises that our individual welfare is assured by an unseen spirit, now and forever, have no moral content. Even if we regard the threats/promises as an enforcement more than an attraction, the moral value is missing.

The second set of religious beliefs is more concerned with social needs, the moral and ethical guidelines that are required in any group situation. And the same powerful spirit who provided for our welfare as individuals, now gives us the behavioral guidelines for our society. Some of the guidelines came from the church hierarchy, but if not directly from a supreme being then presumably by his inspiration or with his assent. So in our case, the Ten Commandments were only a beginning and many of our social values and relationships now have a religious orientation or overlay based on the beliefs of the clergy. Our eating habits, sexual mores, the dress code, marital arrangements, educational curricula, and other areas of our lives are influenced or dictated by religious considerations.

The guidelines for social behavior may be concerned with moral values, but often are from the perspective of a particular religion rather than in terms of human goodness in a fundamental form. The Catholic stipulation that it is a mortal sin to miss church on Sunday, for example, has no moral value beyond the obvious self-interest of the Church.

In the overall scheme of things, then, religious beliefs may serve the emotional needs of the people and the interests of the Church, but many religious beliefs have little to do with promoting an ideal of human behavior. Or better put, the ethical and moral guidelines offered by religion are often overwhelmed by the attention given to miraculous happenings, guarantees of personal advantage and the interests of the Church as an institution. The Christian ethic has been lost in the miasma. And we are reminded of Nietzsche's words that: "In truth, there was only one Christian, and he died on the cross."[2]

There is a case to be made, certainly, that the long-term interests of religion are better served by a closer association with human goodness. There is an opportunity for religion to appeal to the basic goodness in humans and to attract followers by the morality of its position and the force of its example. And the concept of religion as a Disney World of good and evil spirits and miraculous happenings is drawing to a close in any case. Many scientists and theologians no longer believe the two-thousand-year-old tales that have become entwined with a belief in the goodness of Christ. These men and women represent a changing of the guard before the gates of Christianity.

NOTES

1. Andrew Dickson White, *A History of the Warfare of Science with Theology in Christendom,* vol. 1 (New York: D. Appleton-Century Company, 1936), p. 25.

2. Walter Kaufmann, *Nietzsche: Philosopher, Psychologist, Antichrist,* 4th ed. (Princeton, N.J.: Princeton University Press, 1974), p. 337.

Appendix

Science versus Religion in 1990

he following pages summarize how science and religion view matters in 1990, based on a limited survey which compares the opinions of two groups of university professors, totaling 191 professors of anthropology (the science of humankind) and 333 professors of theology (the study of God). The results are not intended to be representative of all professors in the two fields—they reflect only the opinions of those who chose to participate in the survey.

The professors were asked about subjects which represent the substance of Christian beliefs, and related religious ideas:

- A Supreme Being
- Human-Gods
- Prophecy
- Holy Books
- Sacrifice
- Miracles
- Circumcision
- Communion
- Baptism
- Exorcism

- Prayer   • Asceticism
- Faith Healing   • The Soul

Clearly, today's anthropologists and theologians have very different views on religion, beginning with the existence of God and extending to many beliefs that are commonplace in our culture. The survey also notes a number of significant differences between Protestant and Catholic theologians.

Overall, it appears that many Christian religious beliefs have changed markedly from earlier centuries on such subjects as the efficacy of exorcism, the probability of miracles, the value of asceticism, and more. So the character of Christianity has undergone change and promises to change more as we come to a better understanding of the human condition.

A BELIEF IN GOD(S)

	Professors of Anthropology	Professors of Theology Protestant	Catholic
Opinions about the existence of a god(s):			
Believe there is a god(s)	22%	95%	97%
It is impossible to know	33	2	2
There is no so-called god(s)	31	1	1
Do not know/no answer	14	2	—
God(s) and devil(s) are active in this world:			
Spirits can affect our lives	17%	87%	83%
It is impossible to know	21	6	5
Spirits do not intervene	49	3	6
Do not know/no answer	13	4	6

The existence of a god(s) is acknowledged by virtually all theologians, but by relatively few anthropologists, who either reject the idea of a god(s) or suggest that it is impossible to know. Thus the majority of anthropologists are by definition either atheists or agnostics. Among Americans in general, polls show that approximately 95 percent of the American public believes in God.

A somewhat smaller percentage of all professors—both of theology and anthropology—believe that spirits play an active role in the world and intervene in the affairs of humans.

A BELIEF IN HUMAN GODS

	Professors of Anthropology	Professors of Theology Protestant	Catholic
Believe these men were (or are) living gods:			
Brahmin Priests	4%	3%	1%
Emperor of Japan	4	3	2
The Dalai Llama	6	5	3
Gautama Buddha	7	6	7
Jesus Christ	17	92	93

At the time of Christ the idea of an incarnate god was not unusual. Still, the belief in Christ's divinity was not accepted either by the Jewish religious establishment or the Roman government at the time—only Christ's disciples believed that he was the Son of God. Later, after Christianity became the state religion of the Roman Empire, Christ was officially proclaimed the Son of God by the Roman authorities. The divinity of Christ remains a point of contention for Muslims and Jews, who recognize Christ as a prophet and leader, but not as an incarnate human god.

In our culture, at this time, professors of anthropology are not persuaded that humans ever have or can become gods. Christian professors of theology believe in the divinity of Christ but not in the claims of other religions. There is, of course, no scientific evidence to support a claim for or against the possibility of someone becoming a human god.

A BELIEF IN PROPHECY

	Professors of Anthropology	Professors of Theology Protestant	Catholic
Yes—these *ancient* persons were true prophets:			
The Egyptian Prophets	9%	6%	17%
Zoroaster	11	11	19
Muhammad	17	12	34
Abraham	18	86	82
Moses	20	92	91
The Hebrew Prophets	20	92	88
Jesus Christ	21	92	91
Yes—these *modern* persons were (or are) true prophets:			
Billy Sunday	2%	10%	2%
Jimmy Swaggart	3	5	1
Ayatollah Khomeini	3	2	3
Oral Roberts	4	6	1
Pope John Paul	5	13	23
Billy Graham	5	13	23
Mahatma Gandhi	9	14	34

Today, science and religion differ on the concept of prophecy—that is, whether a god(s) has spoken to and through certain men and women as a way to communicate his wishes to the world.

It is noteworthy that neither anthropologists nor theologians—regardless of their beliefs about ancient prophets—are apt to regard modern personages as true prophets.

A BELIEF IN HOLY BOOKS

	Professors of Anthropology	Professors of Theology	
		Protestant	Catholic

These books are the literal or inspired word of God:

Christian Bible	14%	88%	82%
Jewish Torah	15	75	80
Muslim Quran	12	6	18
Hindu Vedas	9	6	19
Buddhist Scripture	9	7	19

These books are mostly myth or folklore:

Christian Bible	75%	7%	6%
Jewish Torah	73	14	6
Muslim Quran	74	68	28
Hindu Vedas	75	70	29
Buddhist Scripture	73	69	29

Note: Other responses are "don't know" or "no answer."

One of the more remarkable changes in belief has been associated with the Christian Bible. At one time the Bible was viewed as the supreme source of knowledge. Saint Augustine gave words to the belief: "Nothing is to be accepted save on the authority of Scripture, since greater is that authority than all the powers of the human mind."

Not shown, anthropologists and theologians both agree that holy books are subject to human error in their transcription and interpretation. From 70–90 percent believe that errors in transcription are possible, and 90 percent errors in interpretation.

A BELIEF IN SACRIFICE

	Professors of Anthropology	Professors of Theology Protestant	Catholic

God's sacrifice of his Son is understandable and explainable in saving the world from sin:

Yes	18%	80%	71%
No	74	13	22
Don't know/No answer	8	7	7

Today, the sacrifice of children would be viewed as pathological:

Yes	81%	93%	90%
No	7	2	5
Don't know/No answer	12	5	5

In a number of ancient societies it was customary for a king to sacrifice his son in times of national crisis, as a ransom to avenging demons. Some scholars, such as Westermarck, have noted that the Greek Church and the more prominent Fathers of the early Christian Church regarded the death of Christ in the same way, as a ransom paid to the devil on behalf of humanity. Other scholars regard the death of Christ as an atonement offered to God for the sins of humanity, and this is the view that is generally accepted today.

Whichever the reasoning, the Bible contains a number of references to the ancient practice whereby the father sacrificed his son. There is general agreement among all respondents that child sacrifice in our own time would be viewed as pathological.

A BELIEF IN PRAYER

	Professors of Anthropology	Professors of Theology Protestant	Catholic
Prayers of petition are futile— they are only wishful thinking:			
Yes—prayers are futile	61%	4%	6%
No—they are not	24	93	90
Don't know/No answer	15	3	4
Help for an unknown ailment would most likely come from:			
A well-equipped, well-staffed hospital	68%	37%	48%
The healing powers of the body, itself	19	9	13
My own prayers to a supreme deity	3	33	14
The employment of a faith healer	0	0	0
Don't know/No answer	10	21	25

Christian theologians believe, as they have for centuries, in the power of prayer. On the other hand, anthropologists are more apt to characterize prayers of petition as only wishful thinking on the part of the supplicant.

In a corollary question, nevertheless, professors of theology and anthropology tend to agree that help for an unknown ailment would most likely come from a well-equipped, well-staffed hospital.

A BELIEF IN FAITH HEALING

	Professors of Anthropology	Professors of Theology Protestant	Catholic
Faith healing is more hypnosis than getting help from a benevolent spirit:			
Yes	82%	27%	23%
No	6	50	46
Don't know/No answer	12	23	31
In certain locations, such as Lourdes, miracle cures are routinely achieved			
Yes	12%	14%	60%
No	70	65	16
Don't know/No answer	18	21	24

At the present day, theologians are divided on their belief in faith healing. About half of Protestant and Catholic theologians believe that faith healing is mostly suggestion or hypnosis or are undecided—the other half believe that faith healing is a function of help from a benevolent spirit. Most anthropologists believe that the answer lies in the borderland between suggestion and hypnosis.

In a corollary question, only Catholic theologians attribute healing powers to certain locations, such as Lourdes. Neither Protestant theologians nor anthropologists believe that miracle cures are routinely achieved in such locations. At one time, of course, all Christians strongly believed that healing powers were resident in certain waters, or mountains or at certain shrines.

In an earlier question (see "Prayers") it is apparent that "faith healing" would not be the treatment of choice for theologians, given a personal illness.

A BELIEF IN MIRACLES

	Professors of Anthropology	Professors of Theology Protestant	Catholic
Yes—I believe in these *Bible* miracles:			
Jesus turned plain water into wine	8%	77%	60%
God parted the waters of the Red Sea	7	76	42
Winged angels deliver messages to humans	4	55	14
God wrote the Ten Commandments	3	68	18
Jonah lived in the belly of a fish	1	58	12
Yes—I believe in these *other* miracles:			
Buddhist priests could change their shapes	3%	5%	4%
Statues of Catholic saints have shed real blood	2	9	8

The belief in miracles which has characterized Christianity for almost two thousand years now appears to be on the wane. A number of miraculous occurences have been challenged by scientists and are now being questioned by Christian theologians as well—such as the Ten Commandments.

Not shown here, overall, only 67 percent of Catholic theologians believe that miracles can overturn the so-called laws of nature, compared to 83 percent of Protestant professors and 14 percent of anthropologists.

A BELIEF IN CIRCUMCISION

	Professors of Anthropology	Professors of Theology Protestant	Catholic
Male circumcision was a mandate to the Jews, given Abraham by God:			
Yes	7%	80%	48%
No	72	15	31
Don't know/No answer	21	5	21
Circumcision was just a mutilation of the body, used by a number of primitive societies around the world:			
Yes	58%	17%	46%
No	15	69	26
Don't know/No answer	27	14	28

The Jews had practiced circumcision of the male from early in the worship of the patriarchs (the founders of the faith such as Abraham, Isaac, and Jacob) and regarded circumcision as a mandate from God to the Jews, beginning with God's commandment to Abraham (Gen. 17:10, 11).

It is not clear, however, whether the Israelites borrowed the practice of circumcision from the ancient Egyptians, or whether both learned the custom from still more ancient societies. Scholars do believe that the practice was quite ancient and widespread and probably predated Abraham.

Today, there are mixed views on the origin of circumcision. Anthropologists do not believe that circumcision was a mandate given Abraham by God, Catholics tend to be divided on the matter, and Protestants are apt to believe that God did speak to Abraham.

A BELIEF IN COMMUNION

	Professors of Anthropology	Professors of Theology Protestant	Catholic

Transubstantiation is indeed real. Substances such as bread and wine become the body and blood of gods.

Yes	5%	4%	69%
No	91	94	22
Don't Know/No Answer	4	2	9

When people partake of communion they actually absorb the moral and intellectual qualities of the god.

Yes	9%	14%	27%
No	84	84	53
Don't Know/No Answer	7	2	20

In ancient Greece the corn-god and wine-god were represented by bread and wine which, when consumed, let the worshiper share in the divine attributes of the gods. So the idea of transubstantiation was not unknown in the ancient world.

At the present time, transubstantiation is not a concept believed in by anthropologists nor Protestant theologians. The Catholic theologians tend to view transubstantiation as a real event, although many question the idea that the qualities of the god are passed on.

A BELIEF IN BAPTISM

	Professors of Anthropology	Professors of Theology Protestant	Catholic
Baptism is a necessary protection against the devil and demons:			
Yes	4%	10%	22%
No	94	88	68
Don't know/No answer	2	2	10
Baptism is an effective means of removing original / acquired sin:			
Yes	5%	19%	76%
No	90	78	17
Don't know/No answer	5	3	7

The rite of baptism is another belief that has undergone a marked change since the early days of Christianity. For many centuries Christians believed that baptism was a necessary protection against the witches, demons, and fairies. For this and other reasons, the Fathers of the Christian Church believed that baptism was essential. Roman Catholics have held that infants who die without baptism cannot enter Heaven; instead they are destined to stay forever in Limbo. Saint Augustine went further and asserted that unbaptized children would suffer the fires of Hell for all eternity.

Today, the majority of both theologians and anthropologists would agree that baptism is not a necessary defense against the devil. And only Catholic theologians believe that baptism is useful in removing original or acquired sin.

A BELIEF IN EXORCISM

	Professors of Anthropology	Professors of Theology Protestant	Catholic
Evil spirits may inhabit a place, thing or person:			
Yes	13%	73%	57%
No	77	18	20
Don't know/No answer	10	9	23
Some priests have the power to exorcise spirits:			
Yes	10%	44%	58%
No	78	41	19
Don't know/No answer	12	15	23

A significant change has taken place in the opinions of Christian theologians who in past centuries were totally committed to the idea of demonic possession and exorcism. In fact, Christianity owed much of its early popularity to a reputation for effective exorcism. Today Christian theologians are divided on the subject.

The issue is larger than a single religious rite, of course, because it bears on a fundamental aspect of religion: a raison d'être of religion is the existence of evil spirits and the ability of the Church to control them. If offending spirits no longer have to be taken into account, then religion stands to lose some of its supposed value to men and women.

A BELIEF IN ASCETICISM

	Professors of Anthropology	Professors of Theology Protestant	Catholic
Fasting, continence, isolation and pain are pleasing to a god(s):			
Yes	4%	19%	45%
No	86	67	36
Don't know/No answer	10	14	19
The idea that extreme asceticism is now recognizable as masochism is:			
An attempt to "put down" holy people	14%	28%	29%
A premise that deserves consideration	45	35	51
The probable explanation for asceticism	11	5	1
Don't know/No answer	30	32	19

Asceticism is another Christian religious belief that has lost much of its legitimacy in the twentieth century. In earlier times, self-inflicted pain and suffering were taken as evidence of unusual piety and a close communion with God. Many Christian saints built their reputations on a life of asceticism.

There is still some support for asceticism among Catholic theologians, although not to the degree of old. Protestant theologians are even less persuaded of the value of asceticism and the concept has very little validity among anthropologists.

A BELIEF IN A SOUL

	Professors of Anthropology	Professors of Theology	
		Protestant	Catholic

**Every person has a soul
that continues on forever:**

Yes	21%	78%	93%
No	59	15	2
Don't know/No answer	20	7	5

**A person's soul is examined
on a future "judgment day":**

Yes	8%	77%	69%
No	82	18	16
Don't know/No answer	10	5	15

All cultures and civilizations have chosen to speculate on the existence of a soul and in time have reached a working conclusion. In the presence of an unfathomable mystery, humans have chosen to have their own understanding rather than live in a state of perpetual wonder.

Currently, science and religion disagree on the existence of an immortal soul and on the reality of a judgment day. At whatever points science and religion may choose to agree or disagree on the nature of a soul, of course, it would be difficult to fault their conclusions based on considerations of evidence.

References

Berger, Peter L., and Thomas Luckmann. *The Social Construction of Reality*. Garden City, N.Y.: Doubleday, 1966.

Breasted, J. H. *The Development of Religion and Thought in Ancient Egypt*. New York: Morse Lectures, Charles Scribner, 1912.

Budge, Sir E. A. Wallis, *The Book of the Dead*. 3 vols. in 1. New York: Barnes and Noble, 1969.

Campbell, Joseph. *Myths to Live By*. New York: Bantam Books, 1973.

Cavendish, Richard. *Man, Myth and Magic*. New York: Marshall Cavendish Corporation, 1983.

Eerdmans' Handbook to the World's Religions. Grand Rapids: William B. Eerdmans Publishing Co., 1982.

Frazer, James G. *Folklore in the Old Testament*. Abridged edition. New York: Avenel Books, 1988.

———. *The Golden Bough*. 1 vol. Abridged edition. New York: Macmillan Publishing Co., 1922.

Freud, Sigmund. *Civilization and Its Discontents*. New York: W. W. Norton and Company, 1961.

267

Freud, Sigmund. *The Future of an Illusion*. New York: W. W. Norton and Company, 1961.

———. *Moses and Monotheism*. New York: Vintage Books, 1967.

———. *Totem and Taboo*. New York: Vintage Books, 1946.

Funk, Robert W., and Roy W. Hoover. *The Five Gospels: The Search for the Authentic Words of Jesus*. New York: Macmillan Publishing Co., 1993.

Hamilton, Edith. *Mythology*. Boston: Little, Brown and Company, 1942.

Hartland, E. S. *Primitive Paternity*. 2 vols. London: David Nutt, 1909/1910.

Hastings, James, ed. *The Encyclopaedia of Religion and Ethics*. New York: Charles Scribner and Sons, 1951.

Hopfe, Lewis M. *Religions of the World*. New York: Macmillan Publishing Co., 1987.

Kaufmann, Walter. *Nietzsche: Philosopher, Psychologist, Antichrist*. 4th ed. Princeton, N.J.: Princeton University Press, 1974.

Kemper, Rachel H. *Costume*. New York: Newsweek Books, 1977.

La Barre, Weston. *The Ghost Dance*. New York: Doubleday and Company, 1970.

Meek, T. James. *Hebrew Origins*. New York: Harper and Row, 1960.

Montagu, Ashley. *Immortality, Religion and Morals*. New York: Hawthorn Books, 1971.

New Catholic Encyclopedia. New York: McGraw-Hill, 1967.

Radin, Paul. *Primitive Man as a Philosopher*. New York: D. Appleton and Co., 1927.

Robbins, Russell Hope. *The Encyclopedia of Witchcraft and Demonology*. New York: Crown Publishers, 1959.

Rosen, George. *Madness in Society*. New York: Harper and Row, 1969.

U.S. News & World Report. "Who Wrote the Bible?" December 10, 1990.

White, Andrew Dickson. *A History of the Warfare of Science with Theology in Christendom*. 2 vols. New York: D. Appleton-Century Company, 1936.

Woodward, Kenneth L. *Making Saints*. New York: Simon and Shuster, 1990.

Index